the dehydrated gardener

A DESERT DWELLER'S 3-PART GUIDE TO XERISCAPING

WES TILLMAN

contents

introduction

In desert regions like the one I call home — the US
Southwest — we have a distinct environmental landscape
that is unlike any other on the planet. And, contrary to our
collective mental model of a barren, tumbleweed-laden dust-
bowl, deserts are actually teeming with life! It might not
seem like it, but deserts are complex ecosystems that have
distinct needs in order to function. The plants and animals
that can survive, and even thrive, in desert conditions
combine to form a network of life that is as expansive as a
rainforest. The desert is truly an amazing place brimming
with species.

Unfortunately, ever since the era of early Western
colonization and expansion, the Southwest desert (and other
colonized deserts regions) have been harshly misunderstood
and mistreated. British and French colonizers (for example)
had a mental image of a "proper" landscape that resembled
their homes in the Northern European countryside, failing to
recognize the inherent natural beauty of the desert land-

scapes they now inhabited. Species that were never meant to live in the desert environment were forced into it, choking in the hot sun and in their thirst for water. Things like lawns and golf courses in particular are near impossible to sustain in the desert without extra-natural intervention. Once people tried to alter these landscapes to be something they were not, the desert began to suffer.

To this day, many people living in the Southwest insist on having emerald-green lawns, as if trying to rival those of the Scottish highlands, despite the copious amounts of water needed to sustain their artificial ecosystem. To demonstrate the strain of turning a desert region into a green oasis, there is perhaps no better example than a golf course. In California, for example, the average golf course uses more water per day than 2,000 average households, solely to maintain a grassy appearance. In a state with chronic drought problems, grassy green golf courses are a prime example of how forcing deserts to be something that they're not can place a critical strain on a local ecosystem and natural resources. Furthermore, non-native grass species can create botanical monocultures which choke the native species, such as other plants, animals, and insects, and prevent them from accessing the natural environments they need to survive. In the Southwest desert, we have decimated the natural landscape and funneled limited public resources into the maintenance of a non-natural one.

With a changing climate becoming more of a factor in our daily lives, many people are calling into question the necessity of this kind of landscaping. States like California in particular are facing some of the worst wildfires in history, and much of the Southwest has been experiencing record-breaking heat. Southwesterners are feeling the effects of environmental degradation, and many are asking themselves what changes they can make, to live in closer harmony with their environment.

Many Southwesterners also feel that the extensive amounts of water and fertilizers needed for their lawns are a drain on their wallets. Cost of living is going up all over the country, and for many, their home's landscaping is not a priority. In a drought, you're going to be thinking about how to get water for you and your family, not for your lawn. Yet, you also don't want to have a large patch of brown grass on your property, which can be a terrible eyesore. For those who are feeling the sting of water and energy costs, yet still want a beautiful landscape, lawns just don't seem to be a sustainable option anymore.

Luckily, you can do something about both of these factors to reduce the strain on your local ecosystem and your pocketbook. There are state laws that can be put into place about things like golf courses, artificial ski hills, and other drains on resources that raise the cost of living for everyone else. But besides writing to your congressperson, creating petitions, or voting for candidates that propose these kinds of regulations, there's not much you can do to tackle these giant corporations that guzzle resources from regular people. The good news is that you can do something about your own resource usage. You might not be able to get rid of water-inefficient golf courses, but lawns and landscaping are things that average people do have control over, and with the clear affect on native ecosystems and increasingly scarce resources, some are opting to trade in their lawns for something a bit more desert-friendly.

This re-naturalization of desert landscapes is known as "xeriscaping." Xeriscaping is a landscaping technique specific to desertous regions. Xeriscapers research the native species to their area, be it Arizona, New Mexico, Southern California, or any desertous region on the globe for that matter. They try to tailor their own home's landscaping to those ecosystems. Things like planting native species, getting rid of lawns, and creating a self-sufficient garden that doesn't require a lot of water or maintenance to keep alive, are all a part of xeriscaping. By choosing these kinds of landscaping methods, you will be helping your region's ecosystem, tackling things like water shortages and habitat loss, as well as saving money through self-sufficiency.

As a disclaimer of sorts, I wish to mention that this book is written with beginners in mind. While I hope all readers will take valuable tips away, the more experienced desert gardener may skip over basic sections, such as "What are USDA Hardiness Zones?" or "Basic Tools of the Trade." If you're brand new to desert gardening, you're *__exactly__* where you need to be!

In this book, I will be teaching you all about how to xeriscape your property in three parts. First of all, together we will explore xeriscaping as a discipline and outline some of the important tools and native plants involved in the process. We will then talk about the process of lawn removal, detailing how exactly to dig up your lawn in a way that's safe and effective. Lastly, we will deal with "post-lawn" care and how to maintain your new xeriscaped space. At the end of this process, you should have a landscaped property that you can be proud of: One that looks great, is easy on the wallet, and has a positive impact on your environment around you.

part one

PREPARATION

ONE

what is xeriscaping?

WHEN I TALK to folks who are new to xeriscaping, they think xeriscaping simply refers to the removal of someone's green lawn. And it's an easy mistake to make. Xeriscaping sounds an awful lot like "zero"-scaping, as in "zero lawn landscaping." Luckily for us, xeriscaping can (and should) mean so much more than just ripping out your grass and having a front yard that looks like the "July" entry of a lunar calendar. Xeriscaping refers to a system. Specifically, a system of living species which work together symbiotically. So, while the first step of xeriscaping an outdoor space likely will involve the removal of a lawn - there is a lot more to the process than that.

Each biological region has a unique set of characteristics that need to be intentionally considered. For best results, these areas cannot just have any plant species rooted into their soils; they require instead a carefully-curated makeup of plants which interact collaboratively with their climate. In the same way that you wouldn't try to grow vegetables at the bottom of the ocean, some species of plants simply do not make sense for our desert homes. Tailoring plants to their environment ensures that they will naturally get the resources they need, such as adequate amounts of sunlight, water, and proper temperatures. Planting only native plants also increases your plants' pollination capabilities, since they will be compatible with regional insects and their neighboring plants, allowing them to collaborate effectively with other aspects of their environment. In short, native plants are the best way to go to help your garden meet its full potential.

While native planting has taken off all over the world, xeriscaping specifically refers to native planting practices for *desert* or *drought-prone* climates. If you reside in the Southwestern United States and are looking to increase your garden's native plant species, xeriscaping is the method you would use. Xeriscaping takes ecological research about deserts and forms it into a clear plan of action for constructing a garden that is compatible with your environment. By learning xeriscaping, you can transform your monoculture lawn into a thriving ecosystem that will be a haven for native plants, animals, insects, and even you! There are two main aspects to planting within a xeriscaped space: native planting and companion planting. Both of these are essential to the process of xeriscaping and creating a sustainable landscape.

NATIVE PLANTING

Generally-speaking, a native plant is one that has existed in an environment without human intervention. The South-western United States has been inhabited by humans for tens of thousands of years, with plant species likely being moved around the Americas by indigenous peoples. We can surmise some things through fossils, but these can also be unreliable. Thus, the true pre-human landscape of the Southwestern United States is likely lost forever. Thankfully, our goal in xeriscaping is not to reconstruct *the truest, most pure* imagining of what our gardens might have looked like before humans started moving stuff around; rather, we are really just looking for plants that are tried, tested and known to be able to survive with little intervention out here in the desert. So, by finding plants that are biologically suited to high-sun, low-water environments, we can attempt to reconstruct what the native species' makeup might have been (and perhaps create something that might work even better). Xeriscaping creates landscapes where plants and their environments are highly compatible. We will be learning a lot more about native plants in the following chapters.

COMPANION PLANTING

Plants also need to be considered in relation to *one another*. Just like with people, or with ingredients in cooking, some plants work better with each other than do others. Generally plants that are all native to the same area will work fairly well together, but there are some exceptions. Sometimes two plants that are native to the same region still can't be planted right beside each other, because they both have strong root systems. Alternatively, sometimes plants from the other side of the world can work in perfect harmony because they have compatible needs. This is why you should be doing extensive research into the relative compatibility between your plants, not just between them and their environments. Xeriscaping takes these high-sensitivity needs into account, carefully curating a compatible collection of plants. Companion planting is an essential component of your xeriscaped lawn - one that we will discuss at great length throughout the course of this book.

WHY SHOULD YOU TRY XERISCAPING?

We've talked a bit in the introduction about some of the reasons why people are becoming increasingly interested in xeriscaping as a discipline. It offers many amazing benefits, both for you and the environment. In this section, I will go into more detail as to what xeriscaping can really do for you.

Less Water

Since the plants you will be using in your xeriscaping project require less water than the average lawn or general plants, you will likely be using less water to maintain them. This is great news since Southwesterners are some of the biggest spenders on lawn maintenance water. Maintaining a lawn or other non-indigenous landscape can be a huge drain on water in this region, likely causing one to use significantly more water than, say, a lawn owner in the Pacific Northwest. By choosing plants that are used to having less water, you dramatically ease the strain on your water resources, both from a community standpoint and a personal standpoint.

Financial Impact

The first thing you will probably notice after switching to xeriscaping is that your water bill will get less sad to look at. If you water your lawn every single day (or perhaps more than that in the summertime) then a large portion of your water bill is due to your lawn. With the cost of living going up everywhere, most Americans just can't be spending extra money on their water bills for the sake of green lawns, especially during a drought. You will be able to curb your landscaping costs significantly by choosing more drought-adapted plants.

Environmental Impact

Water consumption is a big issue in the sustainability movement. This issue is particularly prevalent in regions without significant fresh water sources. Much of the water in the Southwest comes from the Colorado River or the Rio Grande, putting intense strain on these two rivers, and requiring much water to be shipped or pumped into regions that aren't nearby. These rivers have dwindled in recent years due to increasing water demand, causing significant environmental degradation in their basins. Plus, the energy required to transport and filter water is a significant source of carbon emissions. Accordingly, using less water will help preserve the limited resources in your community and diminish your carbon footprint.

Drought/Disaster Prevention

Speaking of droughts, the Southwest has experienced its fair share. With climate change rearing its ugly head, these droughts are only becoming more and more common. Xeriscaped landscapes, especially those that yield fruits and vegetables, are less vulnerable to these disasters due to their intense resistance to dryness. If you have all desert-adapted plants on your property, they will be far less at risk when droughts inevitably occur, making your garden, and potential food supply, much more secure going forward into the age of climate change.

Local Incentives

Many states in the Southwest offer local incentives to reduce water consumption. Because of the common droughts and water transportation problems, local governments obviously wants people to be using less water, to put less of a strain on regional infrastructure. Sometimes these incentives will be tax-related, trying to encourage people monetarily to find alternative ways of living with less water. Sometimes the incentives will be to provide free tools, resources or information to promote native planting in the state. It's not uncommon to see local jurisdictions simply shelling out money for xeriscaping projects in an effort to promote water savings. Be sure to check what sort of incentives exist at your local level - there's a good chance you can get some help from Uncle Sam if you live in a drought-prone area.

Less Maintenance

Because xeriscaping creates a native plant-based environment, many of these plants will have their needs covered by the local environment. Much of plant maintenance actually comes from people trying to grow non-indigenous plants, and having to supplement the plant's needs through artificial means. This can be through excessive watering, grow lights, indoor planting, and even pesticides. Essentially, growers of non-native plants are attempting to replicate another type of climate for their plants. What grows like a weed somewhere might be impossible to maintain elsewhere.

For example, roses tend to be a very finicky plant for many North Americans. Only the best American gardeners can achieve perfect and bountiful rose bushes. But visit the UK, and you'll see almost every public park and private home has roses growing like wildflowers. The gardeners aren't particularly better, it's just that roses are adapted to a damper, more temperate climate, something which is hard to achieve here. Thus, Brits likely spend far less time on the maintenance of roses and lawns, for the simple reason that these plants have their needs already met by the natural environment. For desert-dwellers, choosing desert-friendly plants will allow you to grow with this same hands-off attitude, with the natural environment doing the bulk of your maintenance for you.

Unique Beauty

We're all used to the traditional landscaping plants like ferns and day lilies. At a certain point, these flowers become a little dull, especially to more seasoned gardeners. If you want to truly create a landscape that is both beautiful and unique, xeriscaping will help you. Thus, your xeriscaped garden will offer not only an environmental benefit, but also a completely new kind of garden that will fascinate visitors, and keep you interested when admiring your beautiful property.

Variety

Have you ever heard it said that "Variety is the spice of life?" Well, it's no more true in life than it is in gardens. Having a wide variety of plants with different shapes, colors, and textures will add a special intrigue to your garden. Once we remove our visually and biologically bland lawns, we will have an entire canvas to visually interesting, varied spaces.

There are two main benefits to a variety-focused approach to gardening. For one, ecosystems need variety to survive. Plants, animals, and insects need each other to survive. Animals need to eat a wide variety of plants to stay healthy, insects need a wide variety of flowers to pollinate, and plants need a wide variety of pollinating activity to continue growing. It is a delicate system of interdependence. Plain grass is the ecological equivalent of a concrete parking lot, as it offers none of these things for our local desert species. Simply implementing more variety will help to keep the local ecosystem thriving.

Secondly, many people simply prefer the aesthetics of a varied ecological landscape to a plain one. Different types of plants offer a unique set of visual stimuli that keep your eye moving throughout the landscape.

Potential for Self-Sufficiency Boost

There is a whole other facet to xeriscaping, which is growing your own fruits and vegetables. Self-sufficient growing aims to decenter the conventional supply chain by supplementing your existing food sources (grocery stores, farmer's markets, etc.) with food you have grown yourself. Xeriscaping is a specific way in which you can boost your self-sufficiency, focusing on fruits and vegetables that are compatible with your local ecosystem. There are many reasons why the self-sufficiency movement has been taking off, and xeriscaping can help with it.

Financial Benefits

Like with saving water, participating in self-sufficient xeriscaping allows you to save lots of money on food.

Depending on how much you are growing, you can go from saving a few dollars on tomatoes each year, to cutting your grocery bill significantly, to going completely off-grid and getting all your food from independent farming. However far you choose to go with your self-sufficient xeriscaping, you can truly save lots of money through growing local, native plants for your family's pantry.

Disaster Protection

Many people getting into self-sufficiency are concerned about increasing food shortages caused by climate change. The global food supply chain is very vulnerable right now, with huge transportation networks that can be easily disrupted by wars, natural disasters and crop failure. Those who grow their own food, or even get *some* of their food through their own growing, are much less vulnerable to global disasters. Xeriscaping self-sufficiency has the added benefit of being much more low-maintenance, and thus requiring less resources. If you are a self-sufficient xeriscaper, you are very well-protected against any environmental or political disasters that might occur.

Environmental Benefits

Food transportation causes a lot of emissions, even more than water. Take a look in your kitchen, and take a global survey of all the foods in your fridge. You may, at any given time, have bananas from Costa Rica, kiwis from New Zealand,

and mangoes from Pakistan. Fruits and vegetables are shipped from all over the world, racking up tons and carbon emissions via freight and trucking fuel. Besides the water savings and ecological benefit, creating xeriscaped vegetable gardens can also reduce global food transportation, easing your carbon footprint, and providing you with local food to eat.

Health Benefits

There are a number of proven health benefits to eating within your local ecosystem, as well as eating locally-grown produce. Seasonal fruits and vegetables grown with minimal pesticides are some of the best additions to a healthy diet. If you switch to self-sufficient, xeriscaped eating, your body will thank you just as much as the environment will.

SOME CHALLENGES TO XERISCAPING

Like any new undertaking, xeriscaping comes with a unique set of challenges. While there are many benefits to xeriscaping, it's important to also be cognizant of some setbacks or roadblocks you might encounter, both internal and external. In this section, I will list some important things you should be aware of before jumping straight into your xeriscaping journey.

. . .

Large Initial Investment

Garden supplies aren't free. Completely revamping your entire landscape can end up costing you a lot of money. Make sure you're aware of all the costs associated, such as tools, soil, gravel, the plants themselves, and other aspects of gardening. Depending on the size of your project, you might even have to hire a contractor to take care of some of the installation for you. However, you should make these calculations against potential savings. Think about how much you spend on water for your lawn per year, or on food if you plan on growing fruits and vegetables, and calculate how much your xeriscaped garden will save you over time. With these calculations, you will be able to see how long your garden will take to pay for itself, and can make your decision accordingly. Remember: Investment now will likely have big returns later!

May Face Backlash From Landlords or HOAs

Unfortunately, not everyone is on board with xeriscaping. Many homeowners associations, private landlords, and property management companies have strict, antiquated laws about what you can and can't grow in your own space. Sometimes there are even lawn requirements in place, obliging everyone in the neighborhood to have a perfectly-manicured lawn, or height restrictions, prohibiting any resident from having plants that exceed a certain height. These laws might get in the way of you xeriscaping your property. If this is the case, you can sometimes appeal these rules, but if that doesn't work, you can attempt to find workarounds that will allow you to have at least some xeriscaping in your life.

Time Commitment

Along with being costly, gardening is also time-consuming, especially when it means massive installations. There will be lots of initial effort required to install your xeriscaped garden. It can be time well-spent, as many people find gardening to be a very fulfilling activity, but if you simply don't have the time to invest initially, xeriscaping might not be for you.

Long Wait for Results

Much like a forest, gardens take a while to fully mature. You may have a garden full of completely mature plants that have already reached their maximum potential. Giving all that up to start fresh with completely new, young plants can mean a pretty big transitional period for your garden. It will likely not look as full right away, and can (in some cases) take up to 2-3 years to reach full maturity. This wait time is also a concern for many aspiring food growers, as they might not see a yield for a while. If you are not willing to go through this long transition process, you should rethink xeriscaping.

Requires You to Give Up Your Lawn

For those who love lawns, xeriscaping might not sound that great. After all, there are some pretty cool things about lawns. They're perfect for relaxing in a lawn chair, or for an outdoor dining table. Like in the film "Heathers," grassy lawns can accommodate a round of croquet with friends, or if you prefer "Wedding Crashers," an intimate game of Thanksgiving tackle football with family. Lawns are also great for dog owners, giving your pet an opportunity to run around and play. So, while there are a number of truly excellent benefits to setting out on this xeriscaping journey, there are also a few reasons you may choose to keep your lawn around.

TWO

plants, tools, and tips

NOW THAT I'VE established the importance and benefits of xeriscaping, I will start getting into the details of how exactly you can begin xeriscaping. In this chapter, I will list some of the most important things you need to get going. First, I will offer a general selection of the most common desert-friendly plants you might consider in your landscaping journey. Next, I will explore essential tools for creating your xeriscaped garden. Lastly, I will give you some miscellaneous tips to better guide you on your own way. By the end of this chapter, you should be ready to start forming your shopping list for all things xeriscaping!

Note: In a subsequent chapter, I will show you even more plants, ones that are specific to your desert region. So hold off an any final plant decision for now!

Arguably, the most important part of your garden is the plants themselves. With xeriscaping we want to choose the best set of plants for your specific desert climate. Some of the plants listed here will be native to the Southwest, whereas some will just be plants that work well in any desert climate. Each of these plants has a unique set of needs and aesthetic qualities that will bring a distinct character to your garden.

SOIL

Before jumping into the plants themselves, it's important to consider soil. Soil is a critical factor in any garden's success (or failure) and should be intentionally considered. Soil, as a general rule of thumb is referring to the top layer of the Earth. Soils come in many varieties and are largely comprised of the dead carbon molecules which results from the natural plant cycle. Leaves and various plant debris, dead grass — these are the sort of things I'm referring to. This dead matter gets turned into nutrients thanks to a collection of bacteria, worms, fungi and more. The "food" that plants retrieve from the soil is in large part due to this symbiotic relationship with other tiny organisms.

Soil is not all created equal. There are three main properties that define a soil type: clay, sand and silt. All soils will have some combination of these three properties. Generally, the most versatile type of soil is known as "loamy," which is a perfect mixture of all three. However, it is rare that us in the desert Southwest will experience a natural, loamy soil. Usually the native soils on our property will be either more "sandy" or more "clay-ey," depending on the region that we reside. This is a key argument for choosing native plants when possible: native plants will have already adapted to the soil type that is found on your property and in your community without artificial interventions.

See the image below for a visual guide of soil classification:

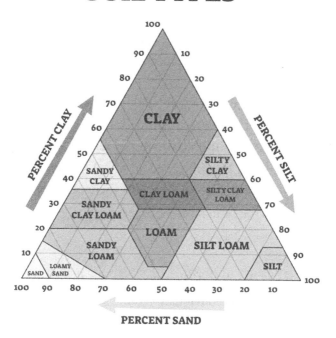

Ch.2, Fig. 1: This chart demonstrates the various soil properties and how they interact. Oftentimes in the Southwest we will have more heavily skewed "sandy" or "clay-ey" soils.

I will be sharing the soil type that is ideal for each of the upcoming plants. One can write an entire book just on soils and the complexity of soil science. This very brief primer will, I hope, help you understand why some plants are best suited for certain regions, but I would encourage you to dive into soil science much more thoroughly if it interests you. A huge inspiration for me is the soil goddess (as far as I'm concerned): Dr. Elaine Ingham. You can find a highly informative YouTube series from one of her courses. In the videos she breaks down soil science in much greater detail. She also has a number of incredible books on the topic.

HARDINESS ZONES (OR USDA HARDINESS ZONES)

Another consideration is your local hardiness zone. A USDA hardiness zone takes into account the soil composition that we just discussed, but it also includes temperature, weather, exposure to light, humidity and so on. A plant that is ideal for your zone will almost certainly thrive even if it is not technically a true-blue native species.

Most of us in the desert Southwest are in the range of 7a to 11a, but there is obviously some deviation from that depending on where you live specifically. Check out the image below to get a sense of your specific zone. Also, please do yourself a favor by looking into the local resources that exist. A local county agent who specializes in agricultural or gardening practices can fill you in on the specifics of your zone, such as watering schedules, frost dates and species that thrive in your area. Also, local universities are a wealth of information when it comes to these factors, so be sure to scour the website of your nearby research institution.

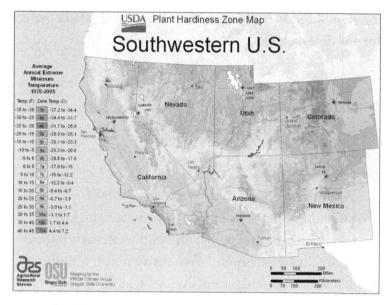

Ch.2, Fig. 2: A map of hardiness zones. Most Southwestern homes are found in the range of zones 7a to 11a.

In addition to soil classifications, I will be sharing the USDA hardiness zone ranges of each forthcoming plant.

TREES

Trees are one of the broadest botanical categories, and can be found in almost all parts of the world, including deserts. So, you have many options for trees that will grow beautifully in your desert garden. The main criteria for a desert-habitable tree are: 1) Water-efficient leaves; 2) Leaves with protective wax; and 3) Strong root systems for water absorption. All of the trees listed here meet these criteria, making them perfect for any desert climate.

Velvet Mesquite

[*Prosopis velutina* | *Zones 9-11* | *Prefers loamy, sandy soil*]

Native to the Southwest. While a number of mesquite variants will thrive in low-water, high-heat conditions, the best option for Southwesterners is the native "velvet mesquite." As a native tree, it is well-adapted to our unique environment, more so than other mesquites (such as the Chilean mesquite). This will help it to withstand external stressors more than its non-native mesquite relatives. Its leaves are high in nitrogen so your soil will get a natural nitrogen treat simply from the leaves that fall to the ground automatically. The velvet mesquite grows to be massive. I have one that grew to about 30 feet! A special bonus: the pea pods that come from a mesquite tree are edible and tasty!

Shingle Oak

[*Quercus imbricaria* | *Zones 5-8* | *Works well in sandy or clay soils*]

This plant is native to parts of the Southwest, although it is also quite common in Midwestern and Southeastern regions. Nonetheless, the shingle oak tree loves the sun and is exceptionally drought-tolerant. These trees grow to heights of 40-60 feet and produce a lot of shade. They also ward off pests in your garden! Easy to grow and easy to transplant if needed.

Desert Ironwood
[*Olneya tesota* | *Zones 9-11* | *Prefers well-drained sandy soils*]

This tree is native to the Sonoran Desert as well as the Baja Californian peninsula. It produces edible flowers and nutritious bean pods (similar to edamame). This tree grows quite large and has been known to grow very quickly out here in the desert!

Hawthorns
[*Crataegus monogyna* | *Zones 5-7* | *Versatile to many soils: sandy, loamy and clay*]

The next tree on this list is also one of the most beautiful. Not native to the desert Southwest specifically, but these trees are highly resilient and drought-tolerant. Hawthorns are particularly noted for their beautiful flowers. This gorgeous tree will add a striking pop of red to your garden, making for a great addition to a colorful garden. Another bonus for bird watchers is the berries that come from these flowers. These berries are not edible for humans, but draw a wide variety of birds to your garden. You'll likely see some amazing creatures enjoying this tree as much as you do. Hawthorns are certainly a great option for any aesthetics-focused xeriscape.

Desert Willow
[*Chilopsis linearis* | *Zones 7-11* | *Versatile to many soils: sandy, loamy and clay*]

If you find yourself in a *very* dry, hot desert region (think, Phoenix or Death Valley) you ought to consider one of the most coveted hot desert trees around. The desert willow, as one could assume from the name, is well-adapted to very harsh environments, will survive long-term droughts and is a beautiful, exotic addition to your space. With blue-green leaves as well as pink flowers, the desert willow will bring color to your yard, and leave you with peace of mind due to its notable resilience.

Shagbark Hickory
[*Carya ovata* | *Zones 4-8* | *Loamy, sandy soils*]

The beautiful yellow foliage of the shagbark hickory is unparalleled, being another great colorful option to add to your xeri-landscape. These trees also have an additional aesthetic (and idiosyncratic) trait: they grow a lovely birch-like bark, which peels like parchment paper.

Maidenhair Tree

[Ginkgo biloba | Zones 5-9 | Versatile to many soils: sandy, loamy and clay]

Translated as "maidenhair tree," the ginkgo biloba is the most ancient tree on this list. Like the shagbark, it also produces exquisite yellow foliage. One of the most distinctive features of the ginkgo is its fan-shaped leaves, making it a unique statement in your garden.

Sunburst Honey Locust

[Gleditsia triacanthos | Zones 3-8 | Versatile to many soils: sandy, loamy and clay]

These are some of the hardiest trees out there, being resistant to truly harsh environments which can range from polluted urban centers to deserts. They have beautiful fern-like leaves, adding a softness to your garden. Although this tree has historically been unpopular for its thorns and messy pods, botanists have made extensive scientific advancements, allowing them to create a genetically-engineered version of the sunburst honey locust that does not have thorns or pods.

Velvet Mesquite

Native to the Southwest and will withstand external stressors more than its non-native mesquite relatives. Its leaves are high in nitrogen so your soil will get a natural nitrogen treat simply from the leaves that fall to the ground automatically.

Shingle Oak

The shingle oak tree loves the sun and is exceptionally drought-tolerant. These trees grow to heights of 40-60 feet and produces a lot of shade.

Desert Ironwood

Native to the Sonoran Desert as well as the Baja Californian peninsula. Produces edible flowers and nutritious bean pods (similar to edamame).

Hawthorn

Seen on the left, the gorgeous flowers that appear on a blooming hawthorn tree. On the right, the (not edible!) berries which will draw a wide variety of birds even when the flowers aren't in bloom.

Desert Willow

As the name might tell you, these trees are extra resilient in dry areas. The left image shows the pink flowers which bloom. The right image shows the unique curviness of the foliage one should expect to see for most of the year. You can expect your desert willow to grow to about 10-15 feet.

Shagbark Hickory

The shagbark hickory grows to become a large and magnificent specimen. Its yellow leaves make this another excellent option for a color-filled xeriscape.

Ginkgo Biloba

A unique and eye-catching option, a healthy ginkgo biloba can grow up to 25–50 feet in height, adorned with beautiful, spiral-shaped leaves.

Sunburst Honey Locust

With lovely fern-like leaves, the sunburst honey locust is also incredibly practical - being one of the most resilitient trees you can possibly choose for your desert space.

SHRUBS

Similar to trees, shrubs are another must-have in any landscaping project. They add fullness to your garden: working as both groundcover, and as shade for other plants. Shrubs can also add a great pop of color or add privacy from your neighbors, making them both a practical and beautiful component to your garden. Here are some shrub species that work particularly well in desert climates.

Netleaf Hackberry
[*Celtis reticulata* | *Zones 5-9* | *Sandy or loamy soils*]

Native to Arizona and a great option for very hot, very dry regions. Without pruning, the hackberry will take off. So if you have a specific shape in mind, make sure to keep an eye on this plant. It'll grow very quickly on you if you're not careful! The Celtis reticulata is deciduous, meaning it will shed its leaves annually. Also, an added bonus: hackberries are edible and quite tasty!

Chuparosa
[*Justicia californica* | *Zones 8-10* | *Prefers loamy, sandy soils*]

Native to the California desert, Arizona and Northern Mexico. The shrub is a great option for

29

very hot, very dry regions. The common name "chu-parosa" literally translates to "red sucker." It's called this because the flowers the shrub produces are red and can be sucked for a sugary treat. The flowers themselves are great to eat as well (especially in salads). You will surely notice an uncanny resemblance to the flavor of cucumbers.

Fairy Duster
[*Calliandra eriophylla* | *Zones 9-12* | *Prefers loamy, sandy soils*]

This shrub has some of the most stunning flowers, ranging from pink to red to orange. Native to the California desert, Arizona and Northern Mexico. You will notice more native birds hanging around your garden after installing this shrub because they eat the flowers like they're going out of style! Bees and butterflies love this plant as well. Calliandra eriophylla is notably drought-tolerant and heat-resistant after it becomes established.

Blue Star Juniper
[*Juniperus squamata* | *Zones 4-8* | *Versatile to many soils: sandy, loamy and clay*]

This tiny but beautiful shrub is a must-have for any compact gardener. Its gorgeous blue color makes it a subtle but pleasing hue in your rainbow of a garden, and it pairs particularly well with golden-colored plants. It is also one of the most drought-tolerant shrubs, making it almost impossible to kill, and likely one of the last holdouts in an environmentally harsh climate.

Virginia Sweetspire

[*Itea virginica* | *Zones 5-10* | *Prefers clay-like or loamy soils*]

When you think of Virginia, I doubt you think of a desert. This plant (like its namesake) is often found in moist and humid climates. Surprisingly though, these plants are especially drought-resistant once they have been established. While they need an average to above-average amount of water when starting out, when they are grown you will be thankful for how forgiving and drought-resistant they can be. A strikingly unique plant, the Virginia sweetspire has two main states: the spiky white flowers of summer, and the beautiful red foliage of fall.

Strelitzia, or "Bird of Paradise"

[*Strelitzia reginae* | *Zones 10-12* | *Works with loamy, sandy soils*]

Known more for their iconic flowers, these shrubs are a perfect desert plant. They are a classic tropical plant that will no doubt be a centerpiece in your garden. They are also huge, growing up to six feet tall, so make sure you give them a space where they have optimal room to grow up! The only drawback to this majestic plant is that it is toxic to cats and dogs, so those with pets be warned!

Cotoneaster (many varieties)

[*Cotoneaster apiculatus*, *Cotoneaster dammeri, etc.* | Zones 4-8 | *Versatile to many soils: sandy, loamy and clay*]

These sprawling bushes are some of the most versatile additions to a xeriscaped garden. They feature red berries that, like hawthorn trees, will add that extra pop of color to your garden. Because of their horizontal nature, they are actually perfect ground-covers, climbing across your garden's floor to create a full, natural cover that is far more locally beneficial than grass.

Netleaf Hackberry

Native to Arizona and a great option for very hot, very dry regions. The fruits are yummy, abundant and a wonderful added bonus. Depending on the region, the leaves can change colors seasonally, sporting a more reddish hue in the autumn.

Chuparosa

Native to the California desert, Arizona and Northern Mexico. The shrub is a great option for very hot, very dry regions. It's common name comes from the red flowers can be sucked for a sugary treat.

Fairy Duster

This shrub has some of the most stunning flowers, ranging from pink to purple to orange. Native to the California desert, Arizona and Northern Mexico.

33

Blue Star Juniper

Incredibly drought-tolerant, with lovely blue hues — the blue star juniper is simply a fantastic option for your space (especially if you're hoping to find a companion for your yellow-colored plants).

Virginia Sweetspire

The Virginia sweetspire has two main states: the spiky white flowers of summer, and the beautiful red foliage of fall — a very resilient, drought-tolerant shrub.

Strelitzia (AKA Bird of Paradise)

Birds and insects love the strelitzia. Please be careful if you have cats and dogs roaming around, otherwise this is a truly magnificent, unique option to fill some space in your drought-tolerant garden.

Cotoneaster

Like the berries of the hawthorn tree, the cotoneaster's berries will give your landscape a fresh splash of color.

CACTI

Of course, the first thing you probably think of when you think of the desert is a cactus. Being one of the most iconic desert plants, and the most closely associated with the region, no desert garden is complete without at least a few cacti. Due to their unique water-storing abilities, cacti are like the camels of the plant world, being able to drink from their long-term water supply for years on end. Peruse this list to find the best cactus for you and your garden.

Beavertail Cactus

[*Opuntia basilaris* | *Zones 8-10* | *Prefers loamy, sandy soils*]

A beautiful round-shaped cactus, the beavertail is one of the classic cactus silhouettes. These plants tend to grow out and not up, growing up to six feet wide. Beavertails are a relative of the general prickly pear cactus (one of the most iconic cacti there is), but the difference here is is that they grow incredible pink flowers (which smell like watermelons). Just be aware that these are a quite prickly variety of cactus, so keep them in an area safe from pets and children, who might get hurt. These guys are also extremely drought-resistant and love dry soil. They can even grow in sand!

(Figure 3, *A beavertail cactus*)

Blue Flame Cactus

[*Myrtillocactus geometrizans* | *Zones 9-11* | *Prefers loamy, sandy soils*]

As its name suggests, blue flame cacti are a wild and uniquely-shaped cactus. The first thing you need to know about these cacti, though, is that they are huge! Growing up to 15 feet high, and about half as wide, blue flames will likely tower over the rest of the plants in your garden, even over some small trees. You'll certainly have a centerpiece here, with not just its size, but its beautiful blue color to draw attention to it. These cacti also sprout beautiful purple fruits, adding even more of a burst of color and interest to their magnificent trunks.

Saguaro Cactus

[*Carnegiea gigantea* | *Zones 8-11* | *Prefers loamy, sandy soils*]

Being the silhouette most people think of when they picture a cactus, the saguaro is undoubtedly a classic. If you want to give your garden a quintessential "wild west" feel, look no further than a simple candelabra cactus. Like the blue flame, they can also grow exceptionally tall, about 10 feet, also making them a great centerpiece to a cactus-focused garden.

Candelabra Cactus

[*Myrtillocactus cochal* | *Zones 9-11* | *Prefers loamy, sandy soils*]

This hardy cactus has a signature look – with its upright, multiple arms curling up like a fancy cande-labrum. The branches are covered in sharp spines that can range in color from pale yellow to deep red. It grows a beautiful white flower at the tip of each arm during the summer months, which attracts bees and other pollinators.

Buckhorn cholla

[*Cylindropuntia acanthocarpa* | *Zones 5-11* | *Prefers loamy, sandy soils*]

A staple of the Sonoran Desert, the buckhorn cholla is native to the Southwest USA. Flowers beautifully and easily in the early spring, and the bud is highly nutritious. The buckhorn cholla is in the sweet spot of prickliness. It is prickly enough to protect itself, but not so intensely prickly that native birds love it and use it as a nesting spot.

Queen of the Night

[*Epiphyllum oxypetalum* | *Zones 10-11* | *Prefers loamy, sandy soils*]

A fascinating and unique plant that produces flowers, but only in the evening. Essentially, it develops flowers at night that are destined to wilt and die off once the sun shows up! A native of Northern Mexico and Southern USA, this cactus will withstand heat and long periods of dryness.

Ocotillo

[*Fouquieria splendens* | *Zones 8-11* | *Prefers loamy, sandy soils*]

I've also heard this cactus referred to as a "candle-wood cactus." It is a plant that is indigenous to the Sonoran Desert (as well as the Colorado Desert and Chihuahuan Desert). I like Fouquieria splendens because it grows uniquely tall and narrow, where many other cacti grow quite wide. It is perfect for tactical areas where you need verticality due to its height. You will notice a lovely bright red flowering for large swaths of the year, from early spring to potentially late-fall depending on the rainfall conditions (It thrives after periods of rain).

Beavertail Cactus

The beavertail is one of the classic cactus silhouettes. They grow beautiful, watermelon-flavored pink flowers. Extremely drought-resistant and love dry soil.

Blue Flame Cactus

Be warned! Growing up to 15 feet high, and about half as wide, blue flames will likely tower over the rest of the plants in your garden, even over some small trees. A very intriguing option if you're looking to bring cacti into your xeriscaped yard.

Candelabra Cactus

The paddles of the candelabra fan out into thin, spiky sheets. Perhaps second to only the saguaro - the candelabra is a classic "wild west" option for your space.

41

Buckhorn cholla
A staple of the Sonoran Desert, the buckhorn cholla is native to the Southwest USA. Flowers beautifully and easily in the early spring, and the bud is highly nutritious.

Queen of the Night
A fascinating and unique plant that flowers, but only in the evening. So it develops flowers at night that are destined to wilt and die off once the sun shows up!

Ocotillo
Indigenous to the Sonoran Desert. I especially like this plant because it grows uniquely tall and narrow, where many other cacti grow quite wide. It is perfect for tactical areas where you need verticality due to its height.

FRUITS AND VEGGIES

For those aspiring farmers out there, you can also find some amazing drought-resistant edible plants that will both create a lovely garden, and feed your family. Depending on how self-sufficient you choose to be, you might find that you are able to cover all or some of your existing food needs with just your garden, especially if you are a big vegetable eater. Here are some of the healthiest and easiest to grow fruits and veggies that will do an amazing job populating your xeriscaped garden.

Swiss Chard
[*Beta vulgaris* | *Zones 3-10* | *versatile soil tolerance, just needs well-drained soil*]

Loaded with too many vitamins and health benefits to list, Swiss chard is a perfect drought-resistant veggie. It is one of the most heart-healthy foods you can eat, and with so much awareness around the benefits of leafy greens, you can really do no wrong. Swiss chard is also compatible with high-sun, low-moisture environments, meaning you and your family can enjoy beautiful harvests of Swiss chard even in the most desert-like climates.

Cowpeas
[*Vigna unguiculata* | *Zones 7-11* | *Prefers loamy, sandy soils*]

A variable species of pea that includes black-eyed peas and pink-eyed peas, cowpeas are some of the most ancient vegetable species known. In fact, they date back to Ancient Greek and Roman times, and have been a historic staple in stews and salads. Furthermore, cowpeas offer both digestive health benefits with their anti-inflammatory and anti-cancer properties, as well as soil health benefits, being natural weed suppressants, especially in desert climates. Not to mention that they are also delicious!

Okra
[*Abelmoschus esculentus* | *Zones 9-12* | *Prefers loamy, sandy soils*]

Although it's not one of the more common vegetables found in stores, okra is an amazingly healthy vegetable that is perfect for drought-prone regions. They are known to be amazingly roasted, and even fried, offering excellent heart-healthy benefits. However, they do tend to be a little finicky, especially with their sensitivity to groundwater. This shouldn't be too much of a problem for those living in intensely desert climates, but you should still make sure they aren't drowning in damp soil by planting them in a particularly dry and sunny part of your garden.

Wolfberry (or Goji Berry)

[*Lycium barbarum* | *Zones 3-10* | *Adaptable to a wide range of soil types*]

Both the wolfberry and the goji berry are non-native to the Southwestern United States. They are native to mountainous regions in Asia, including Tibet and China. However, they perform shockingly well in the desert heat, and they survive in periods of extended drought. Wolfberries and goji berries are a superfood, packing a punch of antioxidants similar to blueberries. Great for your immune system and highly recommended for a healthy addition to smoothies.

Sweet Potato

[*Ipomoea batatas* | *Zones 10-12* | *Prefers loamy, sandy soils*]

It's not a secret to most that sweet potatoes are considered a healthy complex carb. They are preferable to many other forms of carbohydrates due to their nutrient-packed makeup and high fiber content. Many may not know though that the sweet potato is relatively easy to grow in areas of high heat! The sweet potato will in fact thrive in sunny, dry areas such as the Southwestern USA. I grow sweet potatoes every year and am shocked by the high yield.

Corn (or Maize)

[Zea mays | Zones 3-11 | Prefers loamy, sandy soils]

You might already be aware of the fact that corn orig-inated in Mexico. It later was brought to surrounding parts of the Americas, such as South America and Central America. As a resident of the Southwestern USA (a neighbor to its place of origin: Mexico), I find that corn grows incredibly well in my garden, and survives the harshest summer conditions. Please note though: corn does not survive as well in extreme cold, so folks in the high desert will likely not have similar success as folks with more moderate winters.

Cowpeas

Cowpeas offer both digestive health benefits with their anti-inflammatory and anti-cancer properties, as well as soil health benefits, being natural weed suppressants, especially in desert climates.

Swiss Chard

The Swiss chard is one of the most heart-healthy foods you can eat, and with so much awareness around the benefits of leafy greens, you can really do no wrong.

Okra

The okra is an amazingly healthy and versatile vegetable that is perfect for drought-prone regions.

Wolfberry or Goji Berry

Goji berries (wolfberries too) are a superfood, packing a punch of antioxidants similar to blueberries. Great for your immune system and highly recommended for a healthy addition to smoothies.

Sweet Potato

You may be surprised to know that the sweet potato is relatively easy to grow in areas of high heat! The sweet potato will in fact thrive in sunny, dry areas such as the Southwestern USA.

Corn

You might already be aware of the fact that corn originated in Mexico. As a resident of the Southwestern USA I find that corn grows incredibly well in my garden, and survives the harshest summer conditions.

GROUNDCOVERS

Some flowering, some more foliage-based, groundcovers are an essential part of your xeriscaped garden. They form the backbone of your garden. They will provide both fullness and biodiversity, allowing for shade, shelter, and pollination for insects, as well as being excellent companions for a number of other plants. Plus, they look pretty amazing too!

Angelina Sedum, or "Stonecrop"
[*Sedum rupestre* | *Zones 5-9* | *Versatile to many soils: sandy, loamy and clay*]

Also known as "stonecrop," angelina sedum is a spiky plant that looks striking in any garden. Though it does flower with some beautiful chartreuse blooms, its unique foliage will end up being the star of the show. It is one of the fastest-spreading groundcovers out there, making it a perfect choice for those impatient gardeners who want to get their garden looking full right away!

Ice Plant
[*Delosperma* | *Zones 6-10* | *Prefers loamy, sandy soils*]

Boasting some visually-stunning purple flowers, the ice plant is a statement piece, through and through. It is, in fact, specifically known as a popular xeriscaping plant, so those looking to become xeriscaping purists would do well to choose it. However, be warned that this plant is so suited to the desert climate that it is extremely resistant to moisture. Its love for dryness is such that its roots will react very badly to sitting in moisture. Make sure that your region is especially dry, or that you have amazing drainage to ensure the safety of your ice plant.

Candytuft
[*Iberis sempervirens* | *Zones 3-9* | *Prefers loamy, sandy soils*]

If you're interested in the most fascinating blooms you've ever seen, look no further than the candytuft. It has beautiful white flowers that appear like snowflakes or fractals. Its foliage leaves something to be desired, but flower enthusiasts will certainly love it.

Angelina Sedum

Also known as the "stonecrop," angelina sedum is a lovely plant that stands out in any garden. Though it does flower with some beautiful chartreuse blooms, its foliage actually ends up being the star of the show.

Candytuft

It has beautiful white flowers that appear like snowflakes or fractals. Its foliage leaves something to be desired, but flower enthusiasts will certainly love it.

Ice Plant

With purple and pink flowers, the ice plant is a great choice for ground cover in very dry regions. Be warned that this plant is so suited to the desert climate that it is actually very resistant to moisture. Its love for dryness is such that its roots will react very badly to sitting in moisture.

DROUGHT-TOLERANT GRASSES

Despite the focus this book has on removing grassy lawns, there are still some great grass alternatives that are more drought-friendly. Though they don't solve the problem of the minimal biodiversity in lawns, they do use far less water, and generally have a lower impact on the environment. For all those who felt the doubts about giving up your lawn that I listed in Chapter 1, these drought-resistant lawn covers can be a great option to have the best of both worlds.

Buffalo Grass
[*Bouteloua dactyloides* | *Zones 4-8* | *Prefers loamy, sandy soils*]

Requiring very little water to survive, buffalo grass is a great way to reduce your water consumption while still having a flat groundcover to use for running and playing. The lushness of this grass's cover is sometimes even more so than conventional grass, meaning it might even be a step up. Best of all, it requires only a quarter inch of water in the summer, making it very easy on your water bill, and will actually survive on less water if need be. The only thing to watch out for with buffalo grass is its slowness to grow. Because it takes so long to mature from seed, buffalo grass is often installed in chunks of sod. So, if you're installing buffalo grass, make sure to look into this option to avoid the long wait.

Sheep Fescue

[Festuca ovina | Zones 4-8 | Prefers loamy, sandy soils]

This highly unusual grass is unique in that it actually grows in clumps, meaning it isn't ideal for lawn sports. However, if you are interested in a more naturalistic look that will contribute to a unique landscape, then sheep fescue could be the best grass out there. Of course, it is also ideal for xeriscaping, given its very small water intake. It is low maintenance in other ways too, needing only minimal mowing and fertilizing. If you're looking for a low-maintenance, low-water, and visually stunning replacement for regular grass, consider sheep fescue as a choice.

Wheatgrass

[Thinopyrum intermedium | Zones 3-10 | Highly versatile and works with a wide range of soil types]

Though less visually pretty than conventional grass due to its coarser appearance, wheatgrass more than makes up for it in hardiness. It needs very little water to survive, and can be left fairly alone to its own devices. As low-maintenance groundcovers go, wheatgrass is a solid and sustainable option. Plus, they are quite easy to grow from seed, so no need for expensive sod to start your lawn!

Buffalograss

Requiring very little water to survive, buffalograss is a great way to reduce your water consumption while still having a flat ground cover to use for running and playing.

Sheep Fescue

Sheep fescue is unique in that it grows in clumps, meaning that it isn't ideal for lawn sports. However, if you are interested in a more naturalistic look that will contribute to a unique landscape, then sheep fescue could be the best option around.

Wheatgrass

As low-maintenance ground covers go, wheatgrass is a solid and very sustainable option. And of course you can juice it for a healthy treat.

MULCH

No garden is complete without mulch. Mulching your garden helps maintain moisture below the surface, keeping your plants watered for longer. Mulch can be bought artificially and installed amongst your plants, coming in a variety of different textures. It can, however, also be created just using the plants in your garden. Trees will create their own mulch through fallen leaves. If you don't engage in leaf removal, you can actually get your own free mulch by the fallen leaves. Though these can be less controllable and less sightly, they are a much cheaper option than buying mulch. However, whichever kind of mulch you choose, it will offer a great way of protecting and trapping moisture for your plants.

TOOLS

Besides the plants themselves, a gardener is not complete without a solid collection of tools. Xeriscaping is a unique set of disciplines that requires you to have all the right things in place. Though it is a lower maintenance method of gardening, it still requires a lot of planning and initial work to get your garden to where it needs to be. In this section, I will list some of the most important tool categories you will certainly need to start your xeriscaping journey.

Planning Tools

The most important thing about xeriscaping is the planning. Because the xeriscaped garden is designed to do things like save money, optimize sunlight, and use less water, you need to make sure you are implementing all the right strategies in your garden. Here, I will look at all the things you might need to plan your xeriscaped garden.

Research Materials

The good news is that this book is the first of all your planning tools! Doing the proper research about xeriscaping and the right plants to use is the first stage of your planning. The next things you will need will be complete lists of all xeriscap-able plants that you want in your garden. Though this book will give you many options to choose from, you might also choose to explore various websites or research seed sections at the store to come up with all the plants you might want to install, and build them into a refined list based on your space, budget, and taste.

Drawing Materials

Next you will need to figure out where all of your plants will grow. Get some graph paper, pencils, colored pencils, erasers, rulers, protractors, and any other drawing materials you like to use, and start drawing up a plan for your garden. Think of it like an outdoor floor plan. You might even want to try some strategies like cutting out movable scraps of your plants to reposition them, or color-coding different high or low-sun areas.

My secret to the drawing process - I take photos of the landscape I am working on. Then I use an image editing software to make the photo very transparent. I print several copies of the transparent image, and they give me a great way draw on top of the photos to explore lots of different ideas. You can see what I'm talking about on the next image page. This stage is all about exploring your garden's potential and limitations, finally settling on a design you're proud of.

Digging Tools

Once you're settled on your garden's design and have purchased all your plants, you need to start preparing the space for planting. I will talk in Chapter 7 about how to properly tear out your lawn, but in the meantime, let's discuss some of the basic materials you will need to dig the ground, and prepare for your xeriscape.

Spades and Shovels

Any good gardener should have a proper set of spades and shovels. These come in all sizes and shapes. Ideally, you should have at least one hand spade for more precise, low-depth digging, and a large spade for more large-scale digging or plant moving. You can choose what shape works best for your terrain. If you have denser soil, you will likely need a sharper blade, but if you have looser soil, like sand, you will need a deeper blade for scooping.

Make sure you have a good collection of spades that will fit all your digging needs.

Hoes and Rakes

Sometimes your soil needs to be broken up, but not dug. Forks, hoes, rakes, and trowels are all slightly different tools which essentially perform the same task: soil loosening for planting purposes. Some of these tools are also great for weeding. The tool you choose is, again, dependent on the density of your soil. A rake is ideal for smoothing already loose soil, whereas a hoe is ideal for churning the densest of soils. In the same category of digging up sections of dirt and lawn - a personal must-have item for me is an (electric) roto-tiller.

A roto-tiller is going to immensely speed up the "ripping out" part of your xeriscaping journey. While this is the method I always use, please note that roto-tilling can destroy your soil biology, so it should be done only once and only when you're willing to spend some time deliberately restoring the health of your soil afterwards (I will talk more about soils and fertilizing in a later chapter). Most of all, it's important to choose the tools that best suit you and feel right for your space.

Carrying Tools

Gardening involves a lot of heavy objects, such as soil bags, big tools, gravel, and even plants themselves. Xeriscaping in particular involves more extra heavy things like rockery and denser plants. Thus, any good xeriscape needs a plan of action for how to carry these things around, and even transport them between properties. You will likely need both large and small scale transportation plans. For large scale transportation, think about your car's size, and whether or not it can fit all the materials you have planned to use. If not, you might have to rent (or invest in) a trailer. For small-scale transportation, you should have a wheelbarrow to transport bags and plants around your garden, so as not to risk hurting your back. Through investing in strong transportation plans, you save possible injury, and are also likely speed up your gardening process.

Research

There are lots of ways to accumulate inspiration for your specific space. First off, you're doing it right now: reading book like this one will help you find the perfect plants and landscaping for your scenario. Also, a digital tool like **Pinterest** is great because it's a free way to store ideas and to refer back to when you begin the Planning phase.

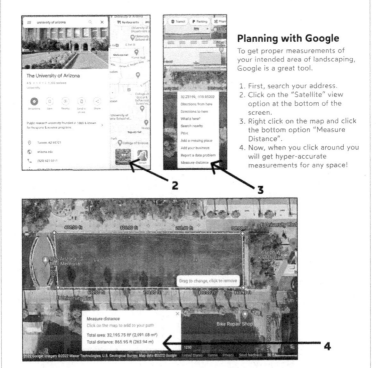

Planning with Google

To get proper measurements of your intended area of landscaping, Google is a great tool.

1. First, search your address.
2. Click on the "Satellite" view option at the bottom of the screen.
3. Right click on the map and click the bottom option "Measure Distance".
4. Now, when you click around you will get hyper-accurate measurements for any space!

Planning with Drawings

When you have measurements and plants that you've settled on, you can start sketching or using design software to begin brainstorming layouts. There are lots of ways to do this, but I prefer the simple method of printing out transparent pictures of the space I'm working on and then drawing directly on top of the transparent image. Print as many pictures as you need. You can't make too many iterations!

You can also print out a full-color (no transparency) image with a blank sheet of paper on top, tracing the image below to create a canvas for your landscaping ideas.

Digging & Carrying Tools

In this chapter we cover the essential digging and carrying tools you'll need. Wheel barrows, sheers and more. Refer back to the section on tools while you're building your first xeriscaping shopping list!

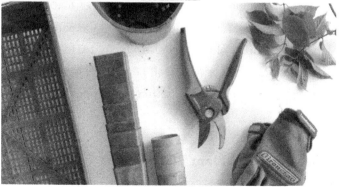

* * *

TIPS ON FIRE RESISTANCE

One of the most unfortunate aspects of drought-prone regions is wildfires. Due to the extreme dryness and heat, desert regions, especially those with a lot of vegetation, are like sitting kindling for fires ready to tear through their landscape. One approach some people tend to take to solve this problem is to purchase plants that are labeled as "fire safe." Although these might sound appealing, there is no scientific proof that such a plant exists, and so there is no real merit in buying plants with this label. You are better off focusing on things like the qualities of the individual plants, and their placement.

Fire-Resistant Plant Qualities

The difficult part about choosing fire-resistant plants for xeriscaping is that many fire-prone qualities in plants are very common in xeriscaping in general. Qualities like waxiness can be fuel to a fire, because of the natural oil in the wax. Density of leaves is also a factor for fire-susceptibility. Thus, it can be a tradeoff between choosing a plant that is ideal for a desert setting, and one that is fire-resistant.

Fire-resistant Plant Placement

One facet gardeners have more control over is the placement of their plants. The best way to combat mass fires is through separation of the plants. You can think of this separation as consisting of distinct clusters of plants which would not be able to brush up against each other should a fire happen. You can even work this kind of clustering into your landscaping, making aesthetic distinctions between them that will serve both the beauty and the safety of the garden. Another important consideration is separating your plants from your house. In the event of a large fire, your plants might catch, but if they are a decent enough distance away from your home, your main structure should at least be spared. If this is an intriguing idea for you, make sure your plants are at least five feet clear of your house to prevent any cross-catching.

THREE

regional cheat sheet

THOUGH THUS FAR I have been treating desert regions as if they were a monolith, this is not actually the case. Xeriscaping can be practiced in a fairly wide variety of drought-prone climates, and you should know exactly which one you are in, so as to practice the right type of xeriscaping. Different regions will all have their own distinct rain patterns, temperature ranges, and levels of sunlight. Thus, you will need to alter your xeriscaping plans to fit your more specific climate range. In this chapter, I will go through five different types of drought-prone climates, and explain the unique aspects of their climate structure and plant needs.

KÖPPEN CLIMATE CLASSIFICATION

The way that I will break down climate regions in this chapter is based on a model known as the "Köppen climate classification." This classification method was developed by Wladimir Köppen in the year 1900 in an attempt to categorize regions by their vegetation. These classifications have helped many a gardener in choosing the right plants for their region, and are still used today in a modified version to determine habitable zones for certain plants. By finding your climate region, you can optimize your plant selection for plants that work best in this region for the best results.

For the purposes of this book, I will be looking mostly at deserts, which encompass a fairly broad category in the Köppen climate classification. Deserts seem uniform, but there are actually a lot of different types of deserts. For a regional category that takes up a third of the world's land surface, it does make sense there would be some variation. A desert is generally defined as a region where rainfall is less than 50 cm per year. Because of their lack of shade and water, animals who do not have adequate water retention abilities, such as large mammals, are generally not found in deserts, instead being populated by smaller, more cold-blooded animals like reptiles. The same goes for plants, though different types of deserts have different kinds of plants that are better suited to them. Through the Köppen climate classification we can see how locations vary, even within desert environments, allowing xeriscaping to become even more accurately targeted than it is.

HOT ARID DESERT

The first desert climate we will be looking at is the hot desert. This region is what many people think of when they think of a desert. Hot deserts see some of the world's highest temperatures. Hot deserts are defined more specifically against the broader desert category as having less than 200mm of precipitation, and a mean yearly temperature of ~65° Fahrenheit. What's amazing is that even though they are not naturally habitable by humans due to their lack of water, feeble farming capabilities, and extreme temperatures, some of the world's biggest cities actually exist in hot desert regions. In this section, I will explore all the qualities of the hot desert, examining how to live in them, and how to grow amazing gardens there.

Regions Covered

So, where are these hot deserts? Well, hot deserts exist in a few distinct places on the globe. The largest by far is the Sahara desert, which encompasses almost all of North Africa, from Morocco to Egypt, as well as most of the Middle East and Arabian Peninsula. There is also a smaller hot desert region in Southern Africa, by Namibia. Australia and South America also have large desert regions. For America, the hot desert regions are predominantly in the Southwest, in the Mojave desert. The states located in hot desert regions are inland Southern California, Southern Nevada, and most of Arizona. If you live in these regions, you should be xeriscaping for a hot desert climate.

(Figure 3.1, *The expanse of a hot arid desert scene*)

Types of Plants

Though it seems like the hot desert climate would not be at all conducive to life, there are many plants that survive very well there, having developed qualities that use the desert's traits to their advantage. Here, I will look at some plants that have the unique qualities needed for growth in hot desert climates.

Plants With Small Leaves

Leaves actually pose some danger in the desert. A process called transpiration causes leaves to lose water through their surface area. One way in which desert plants combat this is through having smaller leaves. The smaller the surface area, the less transpiration can occur, and thus the less water is lost. Plants native to these kinds of desert will therefore

67

often have very small leaves (if they have leaves at all).

Waxy-skinned Plants

Besides being small, there are also other ways in which leaves can reduce transpiration, which is through the coating on their leaves. Desertous plants tend to have waxy surfaces on their leaves and skin. Like mulch, these textures lock moisture below the surface. Often, these same plants will have a rubbery feel, such as aloe vera or other succulents. By "mulching" their own surfaces, waxy-skinned plants avoid losing moisture, and are able to preserve the moisture they do have.

Plants With Spines

Another solution to the transpiration problem is forgoing leaves for spines. This kind of plant structure is usually found in cactuses. These spines will lose much less water than the leaves, preserving your plant and helping it use the landscape to its full potential. If you choose a spined plant like a cactus, you will have one of the hardiest plants in existence.

Plants With Taproots

Going along with the theme of water preservation, root systems are one of the most important parts of a plant's water retention system. Since plants drink through their roots, making sure their root system is conducive to dry temperatures is crucial. A lot can go wrong with roots. Dried roots can lead to a dehydrated plant, and waterlogged roots can get root rot, leading to a droopy and diseased plant. Thus, keeping the roots happy is integral to keeping the plant in general happy. A taproot is a root system that is much longer and runs much deeper than the average root system. By digging so deep, taproots can access groundwater that isn't accessible from the surface. So, plants with taproots might be able to stay hydrated much longer than plants without, making them an ideal choice for drought-prone climates.

Water-storing Plants

Have you ever noticed how gelatinous some succulents or cacti are on the inside? They seem to be made of a sort of goo or gel. Well, in fact, this is one of the distinctive qualities of hot desert plants, holding long-term moisture inside to be used slowly over time. As I said earlier in the book, they are much like camels in that they can survive for long periods without drinking, due to the residual water stored inside their bodies. Pretty amazing plants!

Type of Soil

The soil in a hot desert is not the moist, brown, biodiverse soil most people think of when they image a prototypical garden. This soil has been scorched by the sun, and often evaporated of all moisture by the heat. Thus, in a hot desert, you will likely find crusty, sandy soil that is devoid of water. Though I have mentioned that some distinctive plants have found ways of adapting to this soil, it is still a very harsh landscape where life is mainly survival.

Month-to-Month Guide

Generally, hot deserts have two distinct seasons, summer and winter. Summers are scorchingly hot, ranging between about 90-110° Fahrenheit. The 'winters' aren't exactly frosty wonderlands, but instead a still-warm 65-85° Fahrenheit. For planting during these seasons, there is not much variation, and so you don't have to worry too much about season-to-season differences. However, you do want to avoid the hottest part of the year, June to August, when growing more delicate plants like fruits or vegetables. Thus, planting at the very end of winter and the very end of summer will give you a strong growing season that will be compatible with your climate.

Hot Arid Desert Regional Cheat Sheet

In addition to the drought-resistant plants we discussed in Chapter 2, here we will give you a list of five plants that will thrive best specifically in a hot desert.

Saguaro Cactus
[Carnegiea gigantea]

Though already mentioned earlier — a section on the arid desert would truly be lacking if not for a mention of the saguaro cactus. Perhaps the most iconic hot desert plant there is, this type of cactus is a great addition to any hot desert climate space. It has interesting folds in its surface, which expand and contract, allowing the cactus to hold in a lot of water. For this reason, it is a great drought-resistant option for one of the hottest, driest regions in the world.

Joshua Tree
[*Yucca brevifolia*]

Native to the Mojave desert, Joshua trees are a staple of desert climates. They have a very interesting shape, with arms that feature spiked balls and long claw-like branches. For any gardeners looking to add some height to their landscape, the Joshua tree is one of the best options out there.

Bougainvillea
[*Bougainvillea*]

For a unique option that adds color to your garden, bougainvilleas are a beautiful pink flower. In addition to their vibrant color, they are also a vining plant, which will create a fuller look to your garden. We all know that deserts can look barren if we're not careful, so take this opportunity to fill your garden with low-maintenance pinks and greens. Please note that these plants are only drought-tolerant AFTER they become established. They will need an average to above-average amount of water to get going.

Aloe Vera
[*Aloe barbadensis miller*]

Both a lovely-looking and useful plant, aloe vera is a very popular addition to many xeriscaped gardens. My favorite thing about aloe vera plants is that it literally has healing powers. It can be used to treat sunburns and other skin conditions. Not to mention that drink its juice is delicious and can assist with digestive and inflammation concerns.

Ponderosa Pines
[*Pinus ponderosa*]

If there are any desert-dwellers who want a more northern look to their garden, these rare drought-resistant pines can be a great way to get there. They are in fact native to southern desert regions. Accordingly, they have just the same amount of resilience to heat and dryness as their cactus counterparts.

Joshua Tree

Joshua trees are a staple of desert climates. They have a very interesting shape, with arms that feature spiked balls and long claw-like branches.

Saguaro Cactus

This famous cactus has folds across its surface, which expand and contract, allowing the cactus to hold in a lot of water.

Bougainvilleas

In addition to their vibrant color, bougainvilleas are also a vining plant, which will create a fuller look to your garden.

Aloe Vera

Both a lovely-looking and useful plant, aloe vera is a very popular addition to many xeriscaped gardens.

Ponderosa Pines

Ponderosa pines, are native to southern desert regions. Accordingly, they have just the same amount of resilience to heat and dryness as their cactus counterparts.

COLD ARID DESERT

The words "cold desert" might seem like an oxymoron, but they do exist. Cold deserts are not cold all the time, instead they pair their scorching hot summers and dry conditions with very cold winters. Temperatures in the summer months are the same, but in the winter the temperature can drop below freezing. They tend to exist quite inland and adjacent to hot deserts. Often, they will be found at higher altitudes, or where a hot desert would be if the altitude was lower. In a way, cold deserts actually have harsher climates than hot deserts, since the plants have to adapt to both low and high temperature, as well as dryness. If you live in a cold desert climate, you will have to choose plants that can withstand summer as well as winter temperatures, even snow.

Regions Covered

You can find cold deserts in some interesting places. Much of Eurasia, Southern Russia, and Northern China are considered to be cold desert regions, as well as southern Spain, southern Australia, and parts of eastern South America. In the United States, you will find the largest cold desert just north of the Mojave. In fact, much of western North America is actually considered to be a cold desert, particularly inland: states from Nevada to Kansas, up to Oregon and Washington, and even into Canada's prairie provinces of Alberta and Saskatchewan. If you live in the western half of North America, there's actually a pretty good chance that you live in a cold desert region.

Types of Plants

The plant life of the cold desert looks much different from the plant life of a hot desert. You aren't as likely to see these gel-based water-preservers, since all the water inside would freeze during the winter. Instead, you will mainly see leafy green life like grasses, shrubs, and trees, and only very hardy versions of such. These particular plants have evolved to withstand the harsh climate of the cold desert, and are some of the only types of life that can survive there naturally.

To give you an example of a plant that has found a home in cold arid desert regions, let's explore the class of shrubbery known as the sagebrush (of genus *Artemisia*). These hardy shrubs have adapted to withstand temperatures that drop well below freezing without the need for gel-based water-preservation. Instead, species of sagebrush have developed a deep root system that accesses water from deep underground. Additionally, cold desert plants often rely on other adaptations, like a small size or a low growth habit, to minimize their exposure to the freezing temperatures.

Grasses

The grasses that tend to grow in cold deserts are called bunchgrass. One example of bunchgrass is the sheep fescue I talked about in Chapter 2. This grass uses a form of body-heat sharing, similar to animals who hibernate as families, to preserve both moisture in the dry months, and warmth in the winter months. Through their adaptive qualities, clumpgrasses are able to find ways to maintain both moisture and warmth in the harshness of the cold desert. Finally, a true gem for this region is blue grama (Bouteloua gracilis). Blue Grama is stunning, can be found as far north as Alberta, and is known for its indestructible nature as well as its drought-tolerance.

Shrubs

Like clumpgrasses, shrubs have the advantage of being dense plants that can preserve heat on their own. They work great as groundcovers, and can also help shelter small animals taking refuge from the extreme weather. They are extremely hardy plants that are perfect for a cold desert climate.

Trees

Less common than grasses and shrubs, trees are a more rare find in a cold desert region. However, there are some around. Tamarugo trees (Prosopis tamarugo) and even pistachio trees (Pistacia vera) are conducive to cold desert climates, and both have the added bonus of producing food! Another interesting option is the saxaul tree (Haloxylon ammodendron) which can be found in the high-altitude regions of the Turkestan desert. If you live in a cold desert climate, you have some great tree options at your disposal.

Type of Soil

Like hot deserts, cold deserts tend to have very dry soil, ranging from sandy to salty to rocky. These are not very conducive to life, containing little to no nutrients or moisture. Therefore, the same rules apply as with hot deserts: moisture-preserving plants only. Although the method of water storage differs for cold desert plants. Instead of gel-based water retention like you'd find in an aloe vera plant, the most hardy cold desert plants leverage a deep root system that helps them collect moisture from deep in the earth. Keep this in mind when you're shopping for plants in the cold arid desert.

Month-to-Month Guide

The seasons matter much more in cold deserts than hot deserts. Because of the extreme temperature differences, you have to be very careful when you plant your plants, especially fruits and vegetables. Generally, you should follow the planting pattern of four-season climates, waiting until the last frost is over before planting.

Regional Cheat Sheet

Here, we will give you a list of plants that survive particularly well in cold desert climates.

Rubber Rabbitbrush

[*Ericameria nauseosa*]

This cold desert plant is native to the cold Colorado desert. It is drought-resistant, but has some other attributes that make it more insulated and differentiate it from a typical hot desert plant. It is best grown in acidic or alkaline soil, and you can expect it to bloom from late spring until early fall.

Tufted Saxifrage
[*Saxifraga cespitosa*]

For a floral addition to your xeriscape, consider the delightfully-named tufted saxifrage. It has an interesting quality for a plant: hair. The tufted saxifrage actually grows hair-like leaves which make for a very unique look amongst the rest of your plants in the garden.

Big Sagebrush
[*Artemisia tridentata*]

If there's any gardener who lives at a very high altitude, then the big sagebrush is for you. They are accustomed to heights of up to 10,000 feet above sea level, and will thrive in any mountain or plateau climate. With all of these included benefits, their eye-catching yellow flowers will take the big sagebrush over the top.

Snakeweed
[*Gutierrezia sarothrae*]

This unique plant is a perennial shrub that is notable for its yellow flowers and fan- shaped leaves. It is a great plant for those looking to promote pollination in their garden, as snakeweed attracts a variety of pollinating insects.

Prickly Pear
[*Opuntia*]

Like the big sagebrush, the prickly pear is well-attuned to high altitudes. It does especially well in the high Sonoran desert. This plant is unique for this list because in addition to its colorful flowers, it actually has edible fruit. As the name suggests, it produces pears, which are a purple-red color. Both beautiful and delicious!

Rubber Rabbitbrush

The rubber rabbitbush is native to the cold Colorado desert. It is drought-resistant, and has some other attributes that make it more insulated from a typical hot desert plant.

Big Sagebrush

The big sagebrush is accustomed to heights of up to 10,000 feet above sea level, and will thrive in any mountain or plateau desert climate.

Tufted Saxifrage

For a floral addition to your xeriscape, consider the delightfully-named tufted saxifage. It has an interesting quality for a plant: hair. The tufted saxifrage actually grows hair-like leaves which make for a very unique look amongst the rest of your plants in the garden.

Snakeweed
This unique plant is a perennial shrub that is notable for its yellow flowers and fan- shaped leaves. It is a great plant for those looking to promote pollination in their garden, as snakeweed attracts a variety of pollinating insects.

Prickly Pear
The prickly pear is well-attuned to high altitudes. This plant is unique because in addition to its colorful flowers, it actually has edible fruit.

SEMI-ARID DESERT

A subcategory of desert, the semi-arid desert is a slightly more habitable zone of the desert, often occurring adjacent to arid deserts. Semi-arid deserts also tend to be more rocky than their sandier arid counterparts. Semi-arid deserts will likely be easier to traverse because of this more stable ground. The other major difference between arid and semi-arid deserts is precipitation. Semi-arid deserts get much more precipitation, especially than their hot arid counterparts. They will also not reach the scorching 120+° Fahrenheit heat that hot arid deserts experience. Thus, more life is able to thrive in these regions, even though they are still technically classified as deserts.

Regional Cheat Sheet

Jujube
[Ziziphus jujuba]

If you want some serious height to your garden, you can't do much better than the jujube, which grows to be over 40 feet tall. It can withstand winters, so don't worry if your region has colder winters. It also has beautiful and delicious flowers and fruit for you and your family to enjoy!

Brittlebush
[*Encelia farinosa*]

Don't be fooled by its name... the brittlebush is anything but brittle. It has the ability to thrive in many different climates, including hot deserts as well as semi-arid ones. It is also said to have important uses, both as a type of glue and as a natural type of painkiller.

Triangle-Leaf Bursage
[*Ambrosia deltoidea*]

This interesting plant has a hairy exterior, making it a unique addition to any garden space. It is also a very early plant to flower, starting as soon as February. If you want some distinct character in your xeriscaped garden, the triangle-leaf bursage is a great choice.

Creosote Bush
[*Larrea tridentata*]

This versatile bush can grow in a lot of different kinds of desert climates. It is happiest up to 4,000 feet of elevation, and does very well when growing on slopes. It also has beautiful flowers that will bloom year-round.

Although this plant tends to be somewhat unpopular

because of its smell and difficult growing conditions, it has a lot of useful properties. Once you've grown it, it can last almost a century. It can also be used as an herbal remedy, so many people think that the hardships are worth it.

White Thorn
[*Ceanothus cordulatus*]

One way to bring a rush of life into your garden is with the white thorn, which has a huge wall of white flowers. It is native to California, and will survive in extreme heat (as well as extreme drought). It can also grow extraordinarily well at high altitudes.

Jujube
If you want some serious height to your garden, you can't do much better than the jujube, which grows to be over 40 feet tall. It can withstand winters, so don't worry if your region has colder winters.

Brittlebush
Don't be fooled by its name: The brittlebush is anything but brittle. It has the ability to thrive in many different climates, including hot deserts as well as semi-arid ones.

Triangle-Leaf Bursage
This interesting plant has a hairy exterior, making it a unique addition to any garden space. It is also a very early plant to flower, starting as soon as February.

Creosote Bush

This versatile bush can grow in a lot of different kinds of desert climates. It is happiest up to 4,000 feet of elevation, and does very well when growing on slopes. It also has beautiful flowers that will bloom year-round.

White Thorn

One way to bring a rush of life into your garden is with the white thorn, which has a huge wall of white flowers. It is native to California, and will survive in extreme heat, as well as extreme drought.

COASTAL DESERTS

Although deserts tend to be inland, there is such a thing as a coastal desert as well. They tend to be slightly more humid than dry deserts, as the moist wind from the ocean affects the air. However, they still receive little enough precipitation that they are allowed to be classified as deserts, and they can still be some of the driest regions on earth. The coastal regions of Southern California are an example of a coastal desert.

Regional Cheat Sheet

Chrysothamnus
[*Chrysothamnus viscidiflorus*]

A common plant in the Rockies, chrysothamnus stays very low to the ground. It is able to survive in high altitudes as well as varied temperatures. For anyone living in a coastal region, chrysothamnus is a great option for you.

Black Sage
[*Salvia mellifera*]

One of the larger commitments on this list, black sage can grow up to six feet tall and ten feet wide. If you're planting this one, make sure you have ample room in your garden. It is also native to California, so any Californians looking for a great space-filler in their garden should consider the black sage.

Rice Grass
[*Oryzopsis*]

Simply speaking, this plant is where rice comes from. It can be used as an agricultural plant to, well, harvest large quantities of rice (obviously), but it can also be used in a garden as decoration. The lovely stems and good groundcover can often make this plant just as good a decoration as a crop!

Salt Bush
[*Sarcobatus vermiculatus*]

Native to Australia, the salt bush grows really well in any coastal desert climate. Like the black sage, it is a huge plant, measuring almost 10 feet high and 15 feet wide. Only those with very large gardens should attempt the salt bush, but for those who do, it can really make or break your garden.

Chrysothamnus

A common plant in the Rockies, chrysothamnus stays very low to the ground. It is able to survive in high altitudes as well as varied temperatures.

Black Sage

One of the larger commitments on this list, black sage can grow up to six feet tall and ten feet wide. If you're planting this one, make sure you have ample room in your garden.

Rice Grass

The lovely stems and good groundcover can often make rice grass just as good of a decoration as it is a crop!

Salt Bush

Native to Australia, the salt bush grows really well in any coastal desert climate. Like the black sage, it is a huge plant, measuring almost 10 feet high and 15 feet wide.

MEDITERRANEAN HOT AND WARM SUMMER CLIMATES

A different but comparable climate to that of the desert is the Mediterranean climate. It has wildly different native species and much higher precipitation rates, so it cannot be defined as a desert in the formal sense. However, with recent changes in the climate, Mediterranean climates are becoming increasingly more like deserts, with droughts becoming more common in these regions than ever before. If you live in a Mediterranean climate, you might not necessarily be an ideal candidate for xeriscaping, with there still being many differences between the two regions, but you might still want to look into some xeriscaping concepts, as it will likely become increasingly necessary for you in the coming years.

Regions Covered

Of course, the most obvious region representing the Mediterranean climate is the Mediterranean itself, ranging from Portugal through Tunisia to Turkey. These regions have had famously beautiful weather for most of human history, home to some of the world's most famous civilizations. Yet, there are also regions outside of southern Europe and northern Africa which experience a Mediterranean climate. The west coast of the United States, especially California, experiences a climate that is very Mediterranean in nature. So, if you live in this region, even though you are not in a desert, xeriscaping may start to become more important to you as the climate continues to change.

* * *

Regional Cheat Sheet

Lavender
[*Lavandula angustifolia*]

Starting strong with one of the most popular and
fragrant plants of all, lavender grows perfectly in
Mediterranean climates, particularly famous in the
south of France. You can use lavender for anything
from aromatherapy to tea to cooking. It also comes
with the bonus of its gorgeous purple hue and knack
for covering ground.

Jasmine
[*Jasminum*]

If you want your entire garden to smell absolutely
delightful, well, you certainly won't regret adding
jasmine. It is technically in the olive family, which
explains both its aptitude for the Mediterranean, and
its vining quality. It's gorgeous, delicate flowers are a
great plus as well.

Passion Flower
[*Passiflora*]

This extremely unique-looking flower appears like
an electric shock of purple with its zigzagging

tendrils and striking colors. This flower also grows extremely rapidly, making it great for the impatient gardener, or one who has to fill their garden quickly.

Artemisia
[*Artemisia vulgaris*]

This plant is another with healing powers. Some claim that it has the power to cure malaria. While you probably won't be opening a pharmacy anytime soon, this plant can still add some lovely foliage to your garden with its beautiful curtain of green.

Blue Fescue
[*Festuca glauca*]

Grasses are a great way to cover the ground in your garden. This blue fescue grass is perfect for adding some color while doing that as well. A win-win!

Lavender

Lavender grows perfectly in Mediterranean climates, particularly famous in the south of France. You can use lavender for anything from aromatherapy to tea to cooking.

Jasmine

If you want your entire garden to smell absolutely delightful, well, you certainly won't regret adding jasmine. It's gorgeous, delicate flowers are a great plus as well.

Passion Flower

This extremely unique-looking flower appears like an electric shock of purple with its zigzagging tendrils and striking colors.

Artemisia
This plant is said to have healing powers. Some claim that it has the power to cure malaria. While I am no doctor, I do know this plant will add some lovely foliage to your garden with its beautiful curtain of green.

Blue Fescue
Grasses are a great way to cover the ground in your garden. This blue fescue grass is perfect for adding some color while doing that as well. A win-win!

FOUR

accessorizing and complementing your plants

UP UNTIL NOW, we have talked exclusively about the vegetation side of xeriscaping, but the plants involved are only half the battle. Adding in decorations and structures to your garden is an entirely separate art form that should be planned and perfected. Things like gravel, bird baths, garden walls, rockery, stepping stones, and many other outdoor landscaping materials can be used to add a touch of architecture to your garden. These things are sometimes referred to as 'hardscapes,' or non-living aspects of a garden that contribute to its design. In this chapter, I will be looking at elements which will elevate your garden beyond just a collection of plants, making it into a landscape.

This area might seem like a good place to cheap out. After all, you're making a garden for your plants, not for rocks and pavement. But your plants need something to help make them stand out. You'll also need to move around within your garden, depending on its size. You should choose sturdy and interesting materials on which to do that. Of course, if you

97

want to buy some cheap decorations like gnomes or bird baths, that's fine, but when it comes to foundational, structural additions to your garden, you should be investing in the best. Your garden will thank you for having strong structures on which to rest or climb, and you'll thank yourself for having well-built pathways through your garden. And, as always, it's best to find these materials locally as much as possible. After all, one important aspect to xeriscaping is going green, so you should try to limit your carbon footprint as much as possible during the setup process.

GROUNDCOVERS

In all likelihood, not all parts of your garden will be covered by plants. There will probably be a certain amount of negative space which will need to be intentionally considered. Look back at your original plan, Identify all of the negative spaces between plants. What would you like to see in those spaces? There are several options for this kind of coverage, known as "groundcover." Each has both aesthetic and practical pros and cons depending on the kind of garden you desire. As you read through the options presented here, reflect on what type of atmosphere you want to evoke in your garden. A natural-looking desert landscape? A dramatic rocky bed? A sleek, modern backyard? You can go as far as creating a vision board of xeriscaped gardens you like, and observe what kind of groundcovers they use in their landscaping, to get some inspiration.

Dry Creek Beds

Dry creek beds are a unique feature of gardens, and serve as both drainage and as a beautiful accessory. Although they mostly work to mitigate excess groundwater, allowing it to be channeled through the stones and then drained properly, they can still be used for xeriscaping in areas with rivers or snowfall. You can create an easy dry creek bed with some rocks, making sure to strategically place the bed in a region in need of drainage, and letting it out in a good place to be drained. Generally, dry creek beds are created with landscaping fabric on the bottom for drainage. Then, you place small rocks in the center of the path. Lastly, larger rocks go around the edges to section it off from other areas. You can unleash your creativity, designing curvy paths or little waterfalls, adding to the visual qualities of your dry creek bed. These serve as both a practical drainage solution as well as a stunning groundcover addition to your garden.

Pavement

Often, people will use simple lawn grass as ground coverage. But for desert regions, it can be hard to maintain this, and besides, it doesn't really fit the xeriscaping code of ethics or aesthetics. For those living in desert regions, you will likely have to look towards rockier landscapes. One such option is pavement. At first, this doesn't seem that attractive. After all, you don't want your garden looking like a parking lot... But there are, in fact, some really beautiful ways that you can manipulate pavement to create a much more appealing end-result. You might consider using high-quality paving mixes with interesting colors, or perhaps small rocks embedded into the mixture to create a more dynamic appearance. You can also decorate your pavement yourself, using rakes, drawings, or other added materials onto the wet pavement, so it dries in an interesting pattern. The pavement option for groundcover is best for those looking for a sleeker, more modern garden, as it adds a touch of smoothness which will juxtapose nicely your spiky desertous plants. With the right kind of pavement, you can create a beautiful groundcover that is both conducive to the desert environment, and easy on the eyes.

Sand

What better for a desert garden than to use the very landscape of the desert? Sand makes a great groundcover for a more naturalistic-looking garden. You can either create thin layers of raked flat sand in a Zen garden style, possibly even raking in spiral or wave patterns to match other design aspects of your garden. Alternatively, you can pile your sand up in dunes that create a more rustic desert-inspired look. Both of these options will make for a stunning groundcover. The one disadvantage of sand is that (unless you don't mind your outdoor space looking quite unkempt) it's not the best for walking on. To preserve your natural dunes or raked designs, you will have to avoid these areas just like the areas with your spikiest cactus. Thus, the sand option is more on the aesthetic side of ground covering, and is best used in a hybrid aesthetic, with a more foot-friendly material like pavement, especially for a larger garden plot that requires more moving.

Blocks or Bricks

If you have smaller sections that need ground coverage, you can use things like cement blocks or bricks to add a touch of dynamism to your space. These blocks can be aesthetic, perhaps arranged in an interesting way, or stacked to create a sense of height or architecture to your garden. It's up to you if you want to cement these bricks together, or merely leave them loose because you like how they look as raw materials. Whether you're looking to cover just a little bit of ground, or construct a piece of sculpture to your garden, blocks and bricks can be a great, quick solution.

Gravel

One of the most popular groundcovers, especially in xeriscaping, is gravel. Gravel is like the happy middle between sand and pavement. It provides a rougher texture than pavement, but is easier to walk on than sand. For this reason, gravel has become a staple in many different types of gardening, even in non-desert regions. French gardens, such as the ones at Versailles and The Louvre, employ large swaths of gravel that create beautiful walkways from which to admire the landscaping. You can also get lots of different styles of gravel, from small stones to large ones, and from rough to smooth. You can decide which style of gravel best fits your aesthetic. Generally, for a more naturalistic look, rougher stones would be used. For a sleeker, more modern-looking garden, you should use more polished, rounder stones. You can also create non-walkable designs in gravel, especially with finer stones, using them much like sand. However, for the most part, gravel is noted for its walkability, and is thus best used as a pathway groundcover despite its aesthetic potential.

(Figure 4.1, *Gravel used in a xeriscaped garden*)

Tiles

Lastly, you can always go the more livable route by adding patio sections to your garden. Outdoor tiles are a great groundcover for this option. Tiled patio areas can be used to accommodate tables and chairs or benches (and of course the lounging humans that occupy such things!). They can also be used to section off areas, or perhaps showcase a grouping or two of potted plants. Tiles function very similarly to pavement, giving you a flat surface on which to place aspects of your garden's needs. However, they provide a much more unique and original aesthetic to your garden. From the most basic beige tiles to highly customized, painted ceramic tiles, you can find the style and level of minimalism that works best for you. No matter what, you will likely create something that's more interesting than pavement, and just as useful.

WALKWAYS

Along the same lines as groundcovers, you also need paths on which to walk around (and through) your garden. I've touched on the pathway aspect a bit in the groundcover section, but here I'll look more closely at what kinds of materials can be used to create ideal walkways for your garden.

Paved Paths

Going the cement or tile route, you can create clear pathways that are completely paved over for you to walk through. These types of paths have the advantage of giving you a smooth passageway to walk, bike, or even drive on (if it's wide enough). If you are wheelbarrowing a lot of materials through your garden on a regular basis, paved paths are likely the best option for you to maneuver around your garden. They also have the potential to be really beautiful. There are a million ways you can arrange differently-colored tiles to create a beautiful design that will draw eyes around to all your garden's many features. The only clear disadvantage to a paved path is that it will firmly cut your garden in half. You won't be able to have any crossing plants, because their soil paths will be completely cut off. So, make sure that if you put in a path, you are not cutting off any root systems that you don't want to!

Stepping Stones

If you want a path that is less invasive and more embedded into your garden bed, stepping stones can be a great option. These give you a playful path to walk on without harshly cutting your garden completely in half. They can be either big flat stones, or a spattering of smaller rocks depending on your preference. The most important thing with these types of walkways is to make sure there aren't any spiky plants or things that could scratch up your legs in the vicinity, just to make sure the path is safe. The main disadvantage to these paths is they aren't ideal for wheeling, so if you need to maneuver anything through these paths that aren't human feet, you might have a problem. You can consider maybe even having some paths be paved, and others be made of stepping stones so as to create both wheelable and non-wheelable paths, and creating visual diversity.

(Figure 4.2, *A stony path*)

WALLS

You may need to separate different parts of your garden with upright walls, either for shade or aesthetic reasons. You can use a variety of materials for this, but the most important factors for garden walls are height and opacity. High, opaque walls will cast a lot of shade, depending on the placement of the wall and the time of day. They can be strategically placed to either block light or not to block light, depending

105

on their purpose. If your high wall's purpose is not shade-related, such as to block a neighbor's view of your garden, be sure to calculate the shade pattern so you don't end up blocking sunlight to your important plants. Some of the most popular substances for opaque fences are wood, stucco, and brick. These can all have their own distinct style that will create a new look for your garden. Short or transparent fences are a great way to add separation to areas, or keep out animals without compromising your garden's shade options. Some of the more common materials for transparent fences are chain link, chicken wire, and loosely-built wood, like picketing. These fences are a much softer option, which create barriers without blocking visibility. Whatever you choose, let the fence style reflect the aesthetic and function of your garden alike.

ROCKERY

Especially in a desert garden, having lots of rocks can add a beautifully naturalistic feel to the landscape. Rockery can also have a practical purpose, allowing plants to be stacked, or particularly sun-loving plants to be placed at a higher altitude, completely free from all shade. Introducing some rockery into your garden is a great way to add some texture and height to an otherwise flat landscape. Here, I will look at how both large-scale and small-scale rockery can be used to make your garden look and function wonderfully.

Small Rocks

Smaller rockery is often used for decorative purposes. You can use rocks roughly the size of a basketball to add some texture to your planting areas, and even as groundcover. Depending on their texture, you can stack them to create a more naturalistic-looking height than from a brick wall. Because you're xeriscaping, there are actually succulents that grow from cracks in rocks, so you can try setting up a rock pile that functions more like a planter, with small cactuses and succulents scattered throughout. Different kinds of rocks will also evoke different aesthetics. For a unique, craggy look, consider volcanic rocks, which have interesting colors and plenty of ridges. If you're looking to be a bit more modern, slate materials can be a great way to add layered height while remaining sleek. Whatever your garden's aesthetic, you can create something truly fitting with small-scale rockery.

Boulders

With large-scale rockery (mainly suitable for larger gardens) you can create entirely new worlds. Add some levels to your garden by stacking large boulders on top of one another, maybe even creating cliff faces or waterfalls. You can follow the same principle as with the smaller rock stacks, and have larger cactuses or succulents growing out of the cracks in these boulders. Larger-scale rockery of course comes with some issues, the main one being transportation. You will be limited by how much weight you or your vehicle are able to carry. These boulders can also be dangerous to install, so it's advisable to have a landscaper help you when you're installing them, or if you want to have them moved.

(Figure 4.3, *Decorative stones*)

OTHER ELEMENTS

Besides these foundational aspects of your garden's non-plant elements, there are also some things that are purely for decoration. Your garden, after all, should be a sanctuary that you want to spend time in, and look fondly at. Why not add in some extra decorative details to add an infusion of personality to it? In this section, I will list a few supplementary items that will help you inject some visual beauty and intrigue into your garden.

Seating

What better way to enjoy your garden than sitting right in it? There are a handful of options, depending on your desired type of seating. You can install beautifully ornamental benches made out of wood or wrought-iron, which are as good to look at as they are to sit on. Alternatively, for a more comfortable option, you can think about some pillowed lawn furniture for lounging. You might consider installing an eating and barbecuing section to entertain guests in your beautiful xeriscaped space. Just make sure that all seating areas, especially those that might involve fire or cooking, are on a strong foundation, preferably pavement or tile, not sand or gravel, just to avoid any accidents. Sitting in your garden that you have worked so hard to design and install... it doesn't get better than that.

(Figure 4.4, *Example of a seating area in a xeriscaped garden*)

Archways

One way to add some flair and height to your walkways is to introduce an archway to walk under. Since they are more popular in the English garden aesthetic, they can make for an interesting, eclectic juxtaposition within your garden. You can also go for many different types, such as trellis, wire, or perhaps metal poles to create whatever aesthetic your garden is aiming for.

Fake Plants

Yes, the gardener's enemy. Fake plants are something that no self-respecting gardener would want to admit to having, but they do have their benefits. Sometimes, there are spaces to be filled in that don't have access to sunlight or adequate soil, and a few fake plants can work to fill those in. However, being next to real plants can end up emphasizing their fakeness, so be sure to invest in some good-quality, highly realistic-looking fake plants if you are going to incorporate them. The good news is that succulents and cacti already have a fairly plasticy, rubbery surface, which can be much easier to replicate artificially than flower petals. So, if you have some hard-to-reach areas that you want to fill, consider sneaking in some fake plants to close those gaps.

Decorations

Lastly, there are plenty of other miscellaneous decorations you can buy to fill your yard. Think gnomes, statues, abstract sculptures, or any other strictly aesthetic object. Consider implementing some lighting in the form of lanterns, fairy lights, or embedded lamps to add some glow to your garden.

You can even paint murals on your cement or walls to distinguish your own artistic signature within your space. Whatever you do with your garden, make an effort to give it a personal touch that makes the space feel special and unique to you. I personally love to put out bird baths and decorative bowls filled with (unsalted!) peanuts. My neighborhood blue jays stop by daily to say "hello."

Fig. 4.5, Examples of decorative xeriscaped features

HEAT WARNING

One important thing to mention about all these hardscaping features is that they do have a tendency to overheat, especially if they are made of cement, tile, or metal. For this reason, you should consider limiting the amount of ground covered by these materials. Try to break these areas up, or at least offer them some shade from trees or walls, so that you don't end up with a giant terracotta oven in the middle of your garden. In the Arizona heat, where it's possible to fry an egg on the sidewalk, you should make sure that you don't fuel this overheating any more than you need to.

FIVE

warnings and incentives

BEFORE YOU SET sail on your xeriscaping journey, there are some important housekeeping issues and bonuses that you should be aware of. Both good and bad, administrative and legal rules can have an effect on your xeriscaped garden. On the good side, many states offer tax or other kinds of incentives for you to xeriscape your lawn, citing water savings as their primary reason. On the bad side, there are some restrictions you might have to face, mainly due to codes and neighbors. If you go into the xeriscaping process well aware of both the good and bad sides of the paperwork, you'll be able to both avoid any legal snags, and take advantage of any perks. In this chapter, I will list some of the logistical aspects of xeriscaping, helping you plan for your future garden.

WARNINGS

Like all home improvements, there are a number of logistical items that need to be dealt with first before you get into the actual work. Unfortunately, some of these things will be obstacles you simply must pay attention to, so as not to face any violations or lawsuits. There are two main places where these restrictions will come from: the government and your neighbors. On the government side, there are certain codes put in place to protect residents from any unsafe conditions. These things usually have to do with heights, shading cast on public property, and any fire safety codes in place. On the neighbors side, you might be a part of a homeowners association (or HOA), which enforce their own sets of rules dictating what residents can and cannot have on their property. It's important to be aware of these warnings as soon as possible, to avoid any disappointments at elements you won't be able to include in your garden. Here, I have assembled a general list of the things that might pose roadblocks for your garden designing process.

Homeowners Associations (HOAs)

Fairly unique to the United States, but very common in this country, are something called homeowner's associations. In fact, one in five American homeowners is in such an association, so there is a strong likelihood you will be affected by one sooner or later. These associations usually consist of all or most of the residents in a given neighborhood. Their purpose is to create a collective fund and management committee, which oversees common areas and covers their expenses. They are often found in planned communities which have specific resources like swimming pools, private community parks, or even planned community events. To pay for these things, they will charge a monthly fee to all the residents, who also elect leaders to oversee the maintenance of the property. By all accounts, homeowners associations can be a great thing, allowing for the consistent maintenance of community facilities.

However, these associations often also impose rules about the houses in the neighborhood with a particular focus on aesthetics. All are different, but they commonly will restrict landscaping, particularly in the front yard, as well as the appearance of the front of the house, which can affect things like paint color and overall level of maintenance. Some homeowners find these rules very restrictive, citing excessive demands of conformity and an inability to make their own decisions about their own properties. These are the kinds of problems you might run into when starting your xeriscaping journey if you're a part of an HOA.

Lawns in particular tend to be a battleground between HOAs and their residents, with lawns being generally favored by the association. Some HOAs not only require residents to have lawns, but to maintain them to a certain degree, which can cause a lot of water waste in drought-prone regions. Keeping a lawn (much less a green lawn) is becoming less realistic in many areas of the country, and requiring them is putting people at risk. If you are planning to tear out your lawn, you might have to reckon with your HOA. Some people have been denied this right to landscape as they please, with some people reporting harassment from their HOAs for planting things like native butterfly gardens or vegetable gardens.

Here are some ways in which you can fight your HOA to let you ditch the water-guzzling lawn and opt for a xeriscaped garden:

Appeal to the Law

Recently, as I will talk about in the second half of this chapter, state governments have been imposing restrictions on how much HOAs can require, especially in the context of droughts. For example, Texas and California have recently changed their laws so that HOAs are no longer allowed to fine residents for not having green lawns. These rules are a big improvement, and help many sustainable gardeners fight their HOAs for the right to a more environmentally-friendly landscaping method, especially during drought seasons. If your HOA is threatening you with fines for tearing out your lawn, make sure you look into the laws and know your rights.

Rally Other Residents

Homeowners associations are only as powerful as the people in them. You don't always know who is really on the side of the association. You might just have a few controlling people at the top, manipulating dozens of residents who don't care as much about the rules. Consider getting some neighbor friends together, and explaining to them the benefits of xeriscaping, using some material from this book. You might find that they begin to see your point of view, and even have an interest in trying to xeriscape themselves. If you get enough people on your side who approve of xeriscaping, you will have a lot more bargaining power with the HOA higher-ups. As always, there's strength in numbers!

Try to Change the Rules Yourself

HOA rules are made by residents. The rules are not as set in stone as full-blown laws, and can be changed with small amounts of influence. There's no rule that HOAs have to love lawns. In fact, they could even start to go the other way, and start requiring xeriscaping practices instead! Consider going directly to your HOA, and presenting to them some of the benefits of xeriscaping. You can emphasize the low maintenance costs, and the benefit on community drought issues. If they really care about the environment and the expenses of their residents, they might start to see reason and change some of the rules. You can even run for an elected position within the HOA, and try to change the rules from the inside. Remember: You are a homeowner, and your values matter just as much as everyone else's.

Accept Your Restrictions

At a certain point, no matter how hard you fight, you will still run into some restrictions. Short of a complete xeriscaping ban, there are a million workarounds you can come up with to adopt xeriscaping practices without facing fines from your HOA. You can garden in places the HOA doesn't restrict, such as the back yard or indoors. You can install smaller desert-friendly plants that will not exceed height restrictions. If you're required to have a lawn, you can still install some of the more drought-friendly grasses I looked at in Chapter 2. While you might not be able to let your creativity run wild with crazy xeriscaping designs, there are still some ways you can practice xeriscaping values within HOA restrictions.

Objecting Neighbors

Short of HOAs, you might just have neighbors who generally complain about your xeriscaping. This could be an installation issue, since some larger-scale xeriscaping projects take a lot of installing work, which can be noisy and intrusive. But, they might also generally object to what you're doing, citing height, shade, or even eyesore concerns. While they don't have any real power over you, it's not good to have an unpleasant relationship with your neighbors. The first thing you should do to prevent any conflicts is to be upfront about your plans from the beginning, perhaps even providing a detailed map of how and when you plan to install your xeriscaped garden, as well as which plants will be going in. This will make your neighbors feel more involved in the process, and hopefully prevent them from being too angry with you throughout the various steps. This will also give you a lower stakes opportunity to negotiate with them and listen to their concerns. It will be much easier for both of you if your neighbors strike down your giant cactus idea before it's bought, rather than during its installation! Being transparent and accepting criticism are the best ways to keep your neighbors happy during this big transition.

City Codes

The highest form of restrictions that cannot be changed are municipal, state, or even federal codes that restrict certain types of landscaping. Like with homeowners associations, these codes might get in the way of certain ideas you had for your xeriscaped garden. However, unlike HOAs, these rules are punishable by law, and should never be deliberately disobeyed. Government codes are also usually much more about safety and impact on the community than aesthetics. So, because they are designed to help you and your community stay safe, they are worth following both for legal reasons, and for your own personal safety. Things like fire hazards, potential falling zones, and shade cast on community planting ground can all be factors in government codes that limit xeriscapes. You might run into species codes, restricting you from planting certain invasive plants, or plants that are harmful to local animals or insects. Again, always make sure you are aware of all codes that might apply to your garden, so as to not be disappointed further along in the process, or worse, lose money because you have to scrap a plant or a hardscaping feature. It is best not to try to fight these codes, as they are there for a reason, and are much more difficult to appeal than HOA restrictions. Besides, government codes are usually far less restrictive, meaning you will likely still be able to find a way to achieve all your xeriscaping dreams while keeping you and your community safe.

Cost and Labor

As I mentioned earlier, although xeriscaping is a lower-cost and lower-maintenance alternative to conventional gardening, especially lawns, there is still a significant cost of setting it up. You will have to pay for materials, waste removal, and possibly even labor for more high-stakes projects. I will talk a little bit more about preparation in the next chapter, but bear in mind the cost of everything, and make sure you budget your money so you know exactly how much you're spending. Xeriscaping also requires a lot of time to set up. Even if you are hiring people to do most of the labor for you, there will still be lots of planning and overseeing work which you will have to do. Make sure you budget not only money, but also time to work all these things out. Maybe wait until you are at a more low-pressure time in your day-to-day life to take on a project of this size, as it will likely demand more of your time and attention than you think. As always, being prepared and planning ahead is the best way to use your time and money wisely.

Pests

Depending on your area and the type of plants you are installing, you might find that there are some animals and insects that pose a threat to your plants. This is especially true of vegetable gardens, which tend to attract animals more than any other type of plant. Generally, insects like bees and butterflies are good for plants, as they are pollinators. But, there are also insects like aphids and termites who might pose a threat to your plants, giving them diseases or eating away at them. Though you might not want to use pesticides, especially if you are xeriscaping for environmental reasons, since pesticides harm insect populations, you still need to protect your plants. As a proactive measure, do some research into the general pest species of your local area, and try not to install plants that are highly susceptible to these species. Reactively, you should look into both natural and chemical pesticide options to keep your plants safe. These factors might restrict your planning process, but shouldn't be devastating to your xeriscaping journey. I will share with you some tips for pest prevention in Chapter 10!

INCENTIVES

So you've gotten through all the things that might limit your xeriscaping project, let's talk now about some things that might help it along. Much of what I have discussed thus far has also clearly been noticed by governments and politicians alike. Governments at the municipal, state, and federal level have begun to introduce programs that offer tax benefits, protections, and subsidies to xeriscaping projects. Some I have already mentioned—like protecting xeriscapers against HOA restrictions—but there are also many others. In this section, I will look at some of the types of incentives that exist for xeriscaping.

Tax Benefits

Some states actually consider a xeriscaped lawn tax deductible. Because you will be relying less on government services like water, the state will allow you to deduct a certain amount from your taxable income based on your xeriscaped garden. The degrees and methods of measuring these deductions vary, as well as the amounts that are deductible. You also often have to alert the government beforehand, and have your project approved in order to qualify for the tax rebate, meeting certain thresholds for xeriscaping and native planting. All states have their own rules, though, so you should make sure to do some research into your specific state's rules.

For example, Fort Collins, Colorado offers two tax benefits for xeriscaping. The first, known as the Xeriscaping Incentive Program, offers $0.75 in deductions per square foot of xeriscaped land for approved projects. This is a key reason why you should always have your projects approved, because incentives like these will only be available to you if you do so. The second, known as the Native Bonus Rebate, offers an additional $0.25 per square foot for planting at least 80% native Colorado plants. These are just one instance of xeriscaping incentives for one southwestern town, but they provide a good sense of what they might look like in your town. So, before filing your taxes, make sure you've done all the proper research so as not to miss out on any exciting opportunities.

Protections

Some governments offer protections for homeowners who are being limited by HOAs when trying to xeriscape. They also might provide exceptions to some codes if you prove that you are xeriscaping according to guidelines. Because governments value the public safety of the environment over the concerns of private owners, they will usually side with the one xeriscaping. If you are dealing with any angry neighbors or restrictive HOAs, you can always do some more research into laws to find some protection as a xeriscaper.

Subsidies

There are plenty of government subsidies for landscaping projects that benefit the ecological landscape of the state, which often involve a form of xeriscaping. This might seem a little suspicious, especially when you see the amounts in some of these grants, which can range from $500-$50,000. But, when you consider that the costs of many of these projects are relatively high, especially including any labor involved, it starts to make sense. Plus, the government itself often engages in these projects themselves, using their own money for landscape revitalization projects. So, you can think of these grants and subsidies as outsourcing this task to you, letting you do it on your own terms. They are also unable to touch most people's private property, leaving tons of land unaccounted for in terms of green landscaping practices. Thus, they want to encourage as many people as possible to convert their land into environmentally-friendly landscapes. When thought of from this angle, subsidies make perfect sense.

One example of such a subsidy is the Austin, Texas Urban Forest Grant, which offers up to $58,000 to private revitalization projects which show a clear benefit to Austin's forests. This grant has huge potential for the city's forests, but the grant does reflect the cost of such a project. Anyone willing to take it on would be doing both themselves and the environment a favor. The city of Austin also offers a similar grant of up to $3,000 for schools that engage in environmentally-friendly landscaping projects, with an emphasis on water conservation. Lastly, for independent homeowners, Austin offers some free materials, such as mulch and irrigation instructions to those who are looking to start xeriscaping. These projects (and more!) show how xeriscapers have plenty of people on their side rooting for them. If you're looking to start a xeriscaped garden, you can look at these benefits, not just for financial support, but for moral support as well. America seems to finally be catching the xeriscaping bug!

SIX

preparation

OKAY, so you're sold on xeriscaping. You've heard about all the benefits, and have already started envisioning your dream landscape. You're all set to start planning your perfect xeriscaped garden. I've already briefly touched on the planning process in earlier passages, but in this chapter I will explore further how the planning process works, taking all aspects into account. By the end of this chapter, you will have a strong sense of what your xeriscaped garden will look like, how much it will cost you, and what kinds of things you'll want to put into it. In short, you will have a much clearer picture of your xeriscaping project!

PLANNING

As I've stated already, planning is one of the most important aspects of xeriscaping. Because of how rigid a lot of the plants are, and how much hardscaping tends to be involved, xeriscaped gardens are less malleable than regular gardens.

You might be able to move the occasional plant, but if you have planned meticulously, all plants should fit only in their proper place. Desert plants also tend to be heavier, pricklier, and generally harder to move than other types of plants. Of course, things like rockery and groundcovers are difficult to move as well. Thus, it is best to be happy with your design beforehand, playing around with a lot of different options before you even get your spade out, just to avoid having to move any of these laborious objects later on.

Brainstorming

This is the stage to get all your ideas out, as well as seek inspiration. For expressing your ideas, try some brain-storming methods like word webs and sketches. Throw out words that you think describe your perfect garden, words like relaxing, dynamic, unique, or rustic. You can also make sketches. This is no time to limit yourself with measurements or budgets. At this stage, just draw your dream garden, disre-garding space. It can be as small as a pot or as big as a national park, as long as it shows off the things you are looking for in an outdoor space. Look back at these sketches and notice things about them. Are you more focused on art and hardscaping? Creating naturalistic environments? Constructing a perfect Zen zone for perfect meditation? Notice what kinds of aesthetics you tend to gravitate towards, and position them at the center of your brain-storming.

Once you've started to get a bit of a sense of what you want, start searching for those kinds of things on Pinterest or

Google images. Save pictures of gardens you like in folders to create a kind of digital vision board. You can also look at gardening books and magazines for inspiration. There are even some really great apps that can identify plants just from a photo, which can be great for quick searches when you're at the plant store. (I personally use a shockingly accurate mobile phone application called "PictureThis" when there's a species I'm unaware of. Highly recommended.)

Again, notice what you like about these pictures. Are you mainly saving pictures of tile work, garden furniture, rockery, or plants themselves? Answering these questions will help guide you in your inspiration. You can also start to look at some of the more practical aspects of these pictures. How did these gardeners pull off this aesthetic? How did they stack stones or layer plants to get that desired effect? Following some xeriscaping blogs can also give you tips in these areas. By letting your imagination and curiosity run wild at this stage, and truly paying attention to what you want, you are accessing the roots of your desires for your space. If you let these root desires guide you every step of the way, you should be able to end up with a final product that you love.

Narrowing it Down

Now is the time to start reeling in your ideas. Take some of the pictures you've saved and think about how they would work in your specific space. Right away, you might have to eliminate anything that's too big for your land, or anything that might be too difficult for you to install or maintain. Start imposing limits on yourself. When looking at each picture that inspires you, start thinking: How would I do this? How much would it cost? Can I commit to this installation and maintenance of this feature? Being truly honest about what's realistic at this stage will help you avoid biting off more than you can chew with your xeriscaping project. Always remember how much time and money this will cost, and make sure you are being realistic with how much you have to give.

Drawing

Once you've created a list of things that are realistic for your space, you can start organizing them. In Chapter 1, I talked about strategies you can use for making these sketches, including cutouts and color coding. Draw upon some of that advice here when starting to sketch up your plans. Remember to keep everything to scale, and be realistic about crowding and shade. You don't want to buy too many plants, and realize that not all of them can fit in your yard!

Photos

Another method to really be able to visualize your new landscaping arrangement is to use an actual photograph of your garden. Try taking an aerial photo of your land, either from a high window, or using an image from Google Earth. These will provide a more realistic look than a drawing. You can then print out the photo, and draw your desired landscape on top of it. There are a few things to make sure of before trying this method. First of all, this works best for landscapes that are already fairly plain. If you have just a flat lawn or paved space, it will be far easier for you to envision your new design on top of it, than if it is already very busily land-scaped. Second of all, you still have to have all the measurements, just to make sure everything is to scale. Take a ruler and draw measurement lines around the edge of the garden, and use that scale to put in your plants. This might involve some complex calculations, so try to have it be a fairly simple scale measurement to avoid confusion, for example 1 foot = 1 inch. This will make it much easier to keep everything properly sized, and avoid any miscalculations. If you have a large garden, this might require a large piece of poster paper. Printing out an aerial photo of your garden is a great way to visualize it, while keeping in mind the realistic look of the landscape, as well as other elements.

Software

There are also some great pieces of software that will help you design your plants. Although this can seem like a more expensive and high-effort option than just drawing, they offer a myriad of benefits. They will make sure everything is rigorously to scale, meaning there will be no mistakes on that front. They also allow you to rearrange things infinitely, making for a much more experiment-friendly design experience. Lastly, they might offer features such as additional plants or hardscaping that you wouldn't have thought of before. Using such software can really help you up your landscaping game. This option is especially useful for those with larger spaces, or who are intent on designing something much more complex. Here, I have compiled a list of four of the best landscaping software that can help you design the best landscape possible.

SmartDraw

This is one of the best 2D landscaping software on the market. It is a very user-friendly software which offers an impressive array of templates. With its simple drag-and-draw landscape, you can design to your heart's content. It also has a feature that allows you to collaborate with other people, meaning you can get lots of input from others on your garden's design. This software is paid, requiring a subscription, so make sure you work the price of the software into your gardening budget. If you want an amazing design that you have the ability to really refine, then it is worth it.

Live Home 3D

If you're really interested in adding height to your garden, and envisioning very clearly what that would look like, then you might want to think about adding in a 3D software. 3D gardening software can be somewhat more complicated to use, and won't necessarily have too many added benefits besides envisioning height, but if these elements are very important for you, they can be worth it. Live home 3D has the added benefit of having architectural features, being both a home and garden design program. So, you can always repurpose it to design some unrelated renovations in your house. This feature can also help you try to match your home's exterior design with your landscape's design, by incorporating your home into the software's rendering. You'll certainly come out with a very cohesive design when using this software. However, the downside of this duality is that it features more interior design features, meaning that you are not getting as wide a variety of exterior features. If you're interested in an all-around design software to create a very cohesive design, then this one's for you. But if you just want to design exteriors, and aren't interested in any of the interior features, you might want to pass on this one.

GardenPuzzle

If you've been using a photo of your garden to design your new landscape, then this software is for you. GardenPuzzle actually lets you upload a photo of your garden, and then use the software's features to design over it. This has all the added benefits of the photo designing method I talked about above, mixed with the software designing method. This design tool is a very simple and easy-to-use interface which will give you a great overview of what you want your garden to look like right on the photo itself. You can also upload photos from their library, which also includes a vast array of plants to choose from. All in all, a solid option for garden designers.

Punch Landscape Design

For the more advanced landscapers out there, Punch Landscape Design offers all the features you would need and more. This software is one of the best on the market and has too many features to mention. One of the most beneficial ones for xeriscaping is a feature that allows you to put in your home's coordinates, which then brings up the topographical data for that region. You can really narrow down your plant searches this way, making your garden the best it can be. It has over 8,000 unique items to choose from, meaning that you will certainly be able to find any kind of plant or hardscaping material you're looking for. It also allows you to design in both 2D and 3D, meaning that all the benefits of the previous software also apply. The only downside to this software is also its biggest strength: Its complexity means that it has a large learning curve when you first start. Those that are tech-savvy will likely catch on quickly, but those that are not might have to leave this one on the shelf. But if you're looking for software that will leave no stone unturned, giving you the best possible landscape designing experience, then go with Punch Landscape Design.

GOALS

The next thing you have to think about when planning your garden is what you want its purpose to be. Are you looking to really save a lot of money through low-maintenance gardening? Are you passionate about climate change and drought-resistance? Do you want to cut down on your family's food budget by growing some of your own? Is your xeriscaped garden meant to be a more authentic sanctuary for your family to enjoy the beauty of your region's flora? In this section, I will explore some of the factors that might come into play when thinking about your garden's purpose. While reading, maybe jot down some ideas to build a mission statement of purpose for your garden.

Financial Objectives

Many people decide to start xeriscaping purely for the savings. They're not wrong to do so. Despite the initial investment, xeriscaping can save you lots of money in water and maintenance costs. This is based on the principle that native plants tend to grow much better on their own than non-native plants. If you're trying to grow non-native plants, especially non-native plants from a very different climate, such as green grass in the desert, half the work you are doing is to artificially create a different climate. Grass is used to rainy climates. By watering your grass frequently in a drought, you are essentially trying to replicate a rainy climate through artificial means. This is why non-native plants take so much energy and materials, because you are constructing a micro-climate that is not native to your landscape. By switching over to native plants, you are not wasting any unnecessary materials and cost on altering the climate.

The other way you can save money with xeriscaping is by planting native fruits and vegetables. If you're able to grow enough to get a good yield, you can supplement your existing fruit and vegetable costs. Depending on how far you want to go, you can actually become completely self-sufficient through this process, especially if you include some livestock. You will have to do a calculation about time versus cost, but almost certainly you will lower your cost of living, and live a little better through growing food you would normally buy. Refer back to our list of drought-friendly fruits and vegetables from Chapter 2 to see what kinds of produce are available to grow in a desert climate.

Environmental Objectives

Another big reason people are interested in xeriscaping is for environmental reasons. If you have strong convictions about things like climate change, water conservation, and animal habitat loss, then xeriscaping is a great way to incorporate combating those things in your daily life. Like I said above, xeriscaped plants require far less materials than non-native plants, and thus require far less water to be maintained. You will be lowering your energy footprint just by reducing your landscape's water and mowing needs. Furthermore, a more varied collection of native plants is very good for the local wildlife. Insect- particularly bee-, loss is rampant in our world today, and planting gardens that help instead of hurt wildlife is integral to their survival. All these things will have a massive effect on your carbon footprint. In addition to this, xeriscaping can be a great way to take back a bit of control. For those concerned about climate change, it can be very easy to feel helpless and overwhelmed. It seems like all the big decisions are in the hands of faceless corporations that don't seem to care about the planet. For the everyday person, it seems like there's nothing you can do. By taking clear action against climate disaster, you are taking back control both literally and metaphorically, doing your part to make a dent in the problem, and assuaging some of your anxiety through action.

Family's Needs

You should also consider your garden's purpose in the context of your family's needs. How do you envision you and your family interacting in the garden? Do you picture all of you spending time in it together, maybe planting new plants, or harvesting vegetables? Or do you imagine eating amazing barbecued meals off a gorgeous patio? How about playing sports on one of your drought-resistant grasses or groundcovers? Before you start designing your garden, really think about what you want to use it for. Think about how you use your garden now and be realistic. You might not realize how much you actually use your lawn until you put in a spiky paradise of succulents and cactuses over it, and realize you can't play catch with your dog anymore. Or, conversely, you might work really hard to preserve your lawn because of an imagined sports-oriented family that you don't really have, thus wasting the opportunity for a crazy creative garden. So, before you start planning, be honest about what your family really wants and needs out of it, and design your landscape accordingly.

Time Budgeting

The last thing you have to consider is how much time you can afford to take. I talked about this a bit in the last chapter in the context of setup, but it's also important to consider the ongoing time commitment. Though xeriscaping is a much more low-maintenance option (you can say goodbye to lawn mowers and constant watering!), not all xeriscaped gardens are made equal. If you are looking to just put in some cactuses and succulents, then you will likely not have to worry too much about time commitment. However, if you are looking to do some more rigorous vegetable gardening, especially self-sufficiency vegetable gardening, then this will likely require a large time commitment. Be honest with yourself about how much you can actually commit to, and don't take on anything that you won't be able to handle.

COST

There are also obvious costs associated with starting your xeriscaping garden. Though these costs will likely not be ongoing, the initial cost is important to consider. There are two main facets to the upfront cost of xeriscaping: materials and labor. Here, I will look at how these two things can add up, and where you should be putting the majority of your money.

Materials

The first thing you will have to spend money on are the elements of the garden themselves. Generally, you can divide costs into two categories: plants and hardscaping. The plant aspect is any living element to your garden, including mosses. You can even include other living elements in this category, like koi fish, or any other living thing you would buy. Hardscaping encompasses any non-living thing in your garden. Obviously, there is a wide variety of cost variation between these two things. You can buy the cheapest or most expensive on the market, and anything in between. Individually, I will break down how much you should spend, depending on your needs.

Plants

Your plants are the heart and soul of your garden. They are the reason you are creating this space. However, it is true that many plants can be very expensive, especially larger plants. If you are buying all your plants full-sized, then this can be a significant initial cost. Buying all adult plants can be ideal if you want to have your garden intact right away, without too much of a growth period to wait for. Yet, you can also save money by buying smaller plants or seeds, and growing them yourself. The good news is that the desert classic succulent is perfect for something called "propagating." Propagating is when you cut up different parts of a plant, and use it to grow a new version of that plant. Succulents and other drought-resistant plants like snake plants are amazing at this feature, and will even do it on their own, unassisted. Thus, many people make small businesses off succulent propagation. You can usually find numerous cheap succulents through online markets for this reason. If you are looking to cut costs in your plant department, scour places like Facebook Marketplace or Craigslist to find people propagating their succulents. You will usually find really reasonably-priced baby succulents that you can then nurture into adulthood. All the benefits of great succulents without the high price tag!

Hardscaping

Because of their somewhat secondary status, the other elements of your garden can seem like the place to cheap out. They don't necessarily have to be high quality, but their quality will still reflect on your plants. Your beautiful cactus might look quite different if it's resting in a majestic clay pot on a beautifully-tiled ground, rather than in a cheap plastic pot on some sloppily-installed pavement. Give your plants the picture frames they deserve by investing in some truly quality hardscaping. This can also be a structural, not just aesthetic, issue. Good quality materials are less likely to break, thus keeping your plants safer. So, while hardscaping can easily be overlooked, there's a lot to be said for investing in good-quality materials. You can also try buying some used, since many people over-buy hardscaping materials and want to get rid of them. Again, look to online markets for some low-priced, high-quality goods.

DIY Versus Professional

The labor aspect of your garden is something where you have a lot more control over the amount you spend. You can either hire someone to do these things, or do them yourself. If you have more intense building—especially involving things like carpentry, brick-laying, or concrete-pouring — it is best to hire a professional. You will get the best value for your money, and won't have to spend months researching proper methods and renting equipment. But, if your needs are fairly simple, and you have some gardening experience as well as the time to spare, save a few dollars by installing yourself.

IRRIGATION

Although desert plants need far less water intervention than other types of plants, irrigation is an important aspect of their growth. Irrigation is essentially the process of piping small amounts of water into the ground, so it can be directly accessed by the roots. It might sound like a lot of work, but it can do wonders for your plants, and actually save you a lot of time watering them. The most popular type of irrigation system is the drip irrigation system. You can even create these systems on a timer, so that they will water your plants at the appropriate times every day, meaning you don't have to worry about any maintenance. Unfortunately, due to the complexity of installing these systems, you will likely have to hire a company to do this. There are many companies that offer package deals on irrigation systems which incorporate installation. Though the cost might initially seem high, it is a very important part of maintaining your xeriscaped landscape, especially in a desert setting. Don't worry; irrigation systems use less water than hose-watering your lawn, so you're still enjoying your water savings!

part two

LAWN REMOVAL

SEVEN

let's do it!
removing your
lawn efficiently

NOW THAT PLANNING'S OVER, let's get to the
action! Once you've planned out your entire garden, it's time
to get into the actual removal of your lawn. Now, not all
readers will necessarily have a lawn to remove. Some of you
might just have a non-xeriscape garden bed, in which case
only some of these roles will apply. If you aren't going to be
removing a lawn, you should still read this chapter, since
there are important steps for landscape removal and preparation that every gardener should know. For those who do have
a lawn, this chapter is absolutely essential reading, as it will
help you both safely and effectively remove your lawn. Over
the course of this chapter, I will take you through all the
necessary steps of removing your lawn, as well as providing
some options for different methods of removal. By the time
you're finished reading, you should be ready to rip out your
lawn, and begin creating your xeriscaped masterpiece!

143

ALL AT ONCE VERSUS LITTLE BY LITTLE

Before I get into the real removal options, I have to talk about the pacing of your lawn removal. There are two major ways people remove their lawns; either all at once on one big gardening day, or little by little. Your decision on how to navigate this will depend on three factors: your time, your tools, and the size of your lawn.

For the first factor, you need to figure out how much time you are able to dedicate to ripping up your lawn. Depending on the size of your lawn, it is possible to do it on a weekend if you are prepared to dedicate essentially one or two full workdays to this task. If so, it's technically feasible in one fell swoop. If you're only able to commit to an hour or so a week of yard work, then you will have to carefully budget out your lawn removal.

The second factor is tools. If you are doing everything by hand, and by yourself, lawn removal can take forever. Consider the method of lawn removal you are doing, and what kinds of tools it would need to speed it up. If you are taking a more laborious method without using industrial-level tools, then you might need to chip away at it.

The last factor, your lawn's size, will really be a consideration in the first two as well. Try removing just one square foot of your lawn, if you can, and multiplying that by the total square footage of the lawn. That will be roughly your time estimate. Obviously, the bigger the lawn, the longer it will take. Create a simple calculation of these three factors:

how much time you have at your disposal, how quick your method is with your tools, and the size of your lawn, to decide whether you want to try to remove your lawn all at once, or in bite-sized chunks.

REMOVAL OPTIONS

Removing a lawn might seem like an easy task. You just rip out the grass, right? But it's actually a very complex process with a lot of different methods, all of which have their own pros and cons. Each method will come at a different speed, require a different amount of skills and materials, and cost a different amount of money. You should look at the kinds of calculations you made in the last section to evaluate what method you should use. As you're reading through these five methods, try to see which one matches up the best with your calculation. That will likely be the method that's best for you.

Option #1: Solarization

One of the most hands-off approaches to lawn removal is one that harnesses the natural powers of the sun, which, in the desert, is a great way to make use of existing resources. The process of solarization is to essentially trap solar heat into the grass using plastic covers, which then kills weeds and grass alike. It's similar to the process of starving out bedbugs, where all water supply is cut off; only with solarization it is also cooked under extreme heat, expediting its dehydration. You can use any plastic tarp that you can buy commercially, and the process takes anywhere from 14-21 days. Through this time, the plastic creates a greenhouse effect, which in turn exaggerates the heat of the sun. In the Arizona or California desert, you can imagine how hot it will get under there, so this process actually works very effectively. But what are the pros and cons?

Pros:

The main pros of the solarization method is that it is fairly easy to do, and requires no expensive materials. Anyone with a plastic sheet and some pegs or bricks can implement this method very easily. For this reason, it also avoids some of the harmful chemicals that are so common in a lot of lawn removal. So, you both save money through the scant materials, and prevent you or nearby animals from being hurt by dangerous chemicals.

Cons:

Solarization also has its downsides. If you are in a rush, solarization is likely not for you. It takes much longer than the average lawn removal tactic, with no results before at least two weeks of waiting. If you are in a hurry to get your lawn out, and don't want to wait even a few weeks, you should consider a different method. Some people also don't like solarization because the plastic covers are an eyesore. You might not like two or three full weeks of walking past a messy-looking plastic tarp over your entire property. You might even get complaints from neighbors or your HOA about the eyesore. If you want to keep your property looking presentable throughout the whole process, then solarization might not be for you.

Option #2: Sheet Covering

This equally-easy and inexpensive method of lawn removal operates on a similar principle to solarization' only, instead of using plastic, it uses cardboard. This method is also intended to "starve out" the grass, creating an air-stifled atmosphere where the grass gets neither the sunlight nor air it needs. The method works by placing wet pieces of cardboard over your recently-mowed grass, then spreading roughly half a foot of mulch over that. This will create a thick layer that is designed to completely trample the grass. The best part is that there is no waste or removal process like there is with solarization. The cardboard eventually breaks down, meaning that you can actually plant right over it. So, let's look at the good and bad sides of this method.

Pros:

This method comes with all the pros of solarization, including low cost of materials and no harmful chemicals. However, sheet covering actually has even more benefits. The first is the one mentioned above: There is no waste because the cardboard decomposes in the earth. For those who are especially concerned about the environment, this is a great zero-waste option that has the added benefit of using recycled materials. Just pick up some used cardboard boxes, and let them decompose into the earth. You're composting while removing at the same time. It's a win-win! The other benefit is related to this composting. Cardboard actually has some added nutrients, such as carbon, which can actually help your plants grow by adding richness to the soil. So, if you're looking for an even greener, even more soil-healthy, alternative to solarization, sheet covering is your best bet.

Cons:

The biggest downside to sheet covering is the wait time. If you shuddered thinking about the two to three week wait for solarization, you'll certainly not be happy with the season-long wait for sheet covering. Because you aren't actually removing your grass under the cardboard, just waiting for it to die and then planting over it, you won't actually be able to plant until everything underneath is fully decomposed, which can take months. So, if you're willing to wait until essentially next season to start your xeriscaping, this can be a great option, but if you're looking to plant right away, then you should probably look for another method.

Option #3: Dig Removal

The most straightforward way to remove grass is to just dig it up, but it is not quite so simple as that. The roots of the grass need to be completely removed, yet the layers of soil containing them are quite important to the process of growth for your next plants. Thus, you face a dilemma of needing to remove the grass's roots, while still maintaining soil. The main solution people create is just to add additional topsoil when you are finished, as well as waiting a little while to make sure the roots are completely dead and won't start growing new grass. The general technique for the digging method of grass removal is first to wet the grass, preferably a few days in advance. This will create moisture in the soil, which will loosen the grass's roots, and make it easier to remove. Once you're ready for removal, take a sharp shovel and cut 10 inch by 10 inch squares in the grass. You will be removing these squares one at a time in order to section off the grass. Repeat this process until you have removed all squares. Depending on how deep you went, you can add some top soil at this time. You can also use motorized tillers, which can really speed up the digging process. However, these do cost significantly more than a shovel, so make sure you account for it in your budget. If you are able to remove all the roots of the grass, then you have a low-cost and (relatively) quick method of lawn removal.

Pros:

The main pro is how little materials you need for this process. If you follow the instructions above exactly, all you need is a shovel, something you likely already have, and some extra soil. Thus, this lawn removal method can be done at a very low cost. The other advantage is its speed. Unlike the solarization and sheet cover method, digging can be done in one day, depending on your available time and size of your lawn. There's no wait time of weeks or months; you can start your planting process very soon after. For the more impatient who are anxious to get their grass out and their xeriscaped plants in, digging is the most time-effective method. Like the solarization and sheet covering method, it also doesn't require any dangerous chemicals. All in all, a very solid option.

Cons:

One of the things that can lead to people not choosing digging as their main method is the labor involved. If you have any mobility issues, back issues, or generally don't want to spend a few days doing hard labor, this option might not be very attractive. One modification for this method is to hire a young neighbor to do it for you, since it is fairly easy and doesn't require professional skills. But if you're intent on doing it yourself, it can be very time-consuming and labor-intensive. There is a lot of leftover waste, with all the dug-up grass. You will have to find some way to get rid of all this discarded grass, which might end up costing you money, or at least a drive to the garbage dump. So, there is some extra element to the digging method that might make people want to choose something else.

Option #4: Vinegar

The first chemical method on our list, vinegar provides a natural option for those who want to poison their grass as a method of killing it. However, vinegar alone will not permanently kill the grass by itself. Instead, you will need a vinegar-based mixture that can be soaked into the grass, thus killing the roots. There are many recipes for such a mixture. You can look up some yourself, as they all have slightly different ingredients, but most list epsom salt and detergent as additional ingredients to help vinegar attack your grass. Once you've created your concoction, you can soak the grass with it as densely as possible. Within a few days, your grass should turn brown and start to die. Once all the grass is dead, you do still have to pull it up to make room for your new plants, but because the roots are dead, you won't have to do quite as much digging as in the pure digging method. If you are looking for a way to kill your grass with natural chemicals, vinegar-based substances are probably the best option.

Pros:

The best thing about this method is that it is both quick, like the digging method, and hands-off, like the solarization method. You won't have to do as much labor as digging, nor wait as long as solarization, so it's the best of both worlds. It is also a great way to use a chemical without using any that involve poison. If some of the mixture makes its way into your groundwater, it's unlikely to kill any animals, or harm your health significantly. Thus, you can trust that this method is a safe one for those looking for chemical lawn removal.

Cons:

Depending on the size of your lawn, you might run into some cost issues. Even though the materials involved are cheap in general, you might end up having to buy a very large quantity of them. Because the roots of the lawn need to be completely soaked in the substance in order to be completely killed, you need gallons and gallons of the stuff. You can combat this by buying the cheapest substances possible, but the costs might still be high. The other con is that the smell might be a problem. Vinegar is very potent, and if you are soaking your entire lawn with it, you might find it will smell very strongly, even from inside your house. You can try to combat this with a strongly-scented detergent, but the vinegar will likely still shine through. The other problem is proximity to other plants. You might have some other plants in your yard that are sensitive to vinegar, which might be accidentally killed in the process. To avoid this, make sure the area where you are killing grass is very isolated, and that none of your other vulnerable plants share the same soil. In general, the risks are moderate for the vinegar method, but might be enough to keep some away.

Option #5: Glyphosate Herbicide

Finally, if you are comfortable using a chemical method which might contain harmful materials, the herbicide glyphosate is probably the best option. Glyphosate attacks almost all kinds of plants, and will target the root systems, working like vinegar, and causing the plant to die from the roots. It is a very harsh process, but works very quickly, making it a favorite amongst gardeners. It will kill a lawn within about two weeks, and might need additional sprays to be completely effective. You simply spray your grass with the substance, and wait for it to work its magic. Although, just like with the vinegar option, you will need to dig up and physically remove the dead grass. Anyone looking for the most straightforward method of lawn removal should consider glyphosate to quickly and effectively get rid of their lawns.

Pros:

Glyphosate's simplicity is really where it shines. The chemical requires no mixing, no special placement, nothing but purchasing and spraying. Those who are not interested in labor-intensive gardening or mixing complicated recipes will enjoy the simplicity of glyphosate's application. Because it is a herbicide designed to kill plants, it will also likely work much better than the vinegar mixture, where you might have more mixed results depending on your brand of vinegar and the recipe you make. Glyphosate is guaranteed to work, and so there will be no ambiguity over your lawn's survival. For those who want a clear and easy way of removing their lawn, glyphosate is ideal.

Cons:

The biggest objection people have to glyphosate is that it is a chemical, which can be dangerous, both for you and for your other plants. Glyphosate can't tell the difference between your lawn and your other plants, and so you run the very serious risk of killing some of your more desirable plants, or even some of your neighbor's plants in the process. For this reason, you should be incredibly careful over where and how you spray. Don't go in big strokes around the lawn, be very close and precise. Some people are also worried about the harm these chemicals might do to them and their family, since they do contain an amount of poison. Make very sure that there is no danger of the chemical getting into your water supply, as this can be catastrophic. You can also wear a gas or N95 mask while applying the chemical, to make sure that you don't ingest any of the chemicals into your system. If you take the necessary precautions, it should be safe, but some people still worry about possible repercussions, making glyphosate a no-go for them.

NEXT STEPS AFTER LAWN REMOVAL

Your work doesn't end once the lawn is gone. After all your grass is dead or removed, you will have to begin steps to prepare for the next stage of your garden: xeriscaping! Depending on your lawn removal method (and the specifics of the garden you are putting in) there will be different types of preparation necessary. Here, I will look at two main things you will have to do to your post- lawn-removal space.

Adding Fertilizer

If you've had a lawn in your space for a long time, then adding fertilizer is essential. Lawns are monocultures which add no diversity to your garden. When starting to xeriscape, you need to re-add some of that diversity. Your space will be especially barren since you have just dug it all up. After this process, you need to start reintroducing nutrients. There are a variety of fertilizers to use, including topsoil that comes with fertilizer mixed in. Think about how many plants you are going to be putting in, and how much nutrients they will need. Xeriscaping-friendly plants are generally more low-maintenance, but things like fruits and vegetables will need more. If your garden is going to be 80% hardscaping, with just some plants in between, then you can afford to put just a little fertilizer. But, if you are trying to put in a whole menagerie complete with trees and a vegetable plot, then you're going to want to get some good fertilizer. Compost and manure are great natural options, but you can also use chemical fertilizer. If you feed your plants, then you can rest assured that they will feed you!

Waiting

As I said, your garden has been deprived of nutrients, and so it will take a little while to replenish. These nutrients are living organisms. You can't just put them in the soil and expect them to work immediately. You have to wait for them to develop a culture and mature properly. Once you've fertilized your lawn, you should wait a matter of weeks before you actually start planting. This will give your fertilizer some time to work its magic, and get ready to enrich all your plants.

Grading and Soil Prep

Grading involves artificially creating layers of different kinds of soil so as to make your soil culture more natural. Most natural soil contains multiple layers of things like sand, clay, mulch, or other types of earth. For your garden to be as authentic and conducive as possible for your xeriscaped plants, you should try your best to grade your soil with different layers. If you have dug your lawn up quite a bit, you will especially have to consider grading to replenish your lost soil. Do some research into the topographical makeup of your region, and do your best to replicate it through soil grading. This might end up being more expensive, but the results in your plants' health will be well-worth it.

Planting

The next stage, of course, is planting. Once all your planning, lawn removal, and fertilization is done, you get to actually start putting in your plants. In the next chapter, I will start talking all about the planting process, preparing you to start putting your xeriscaped garden into practice.

part three

LAWN'S GONE... NOW WHAT??

EIGHT

THE MOMENT you've been waiting for: Finally planting your garden. No doubt you've been burning with ideas that you're eager to implement. Now's your chance. Before you start planting on your own, though, you need to learn how to plant every single type of plant. Every plant has its own unique method of planting that should be learned before you attempt anything. You've likely already chosen all of your plants, and now is the time to get into the specifics of actually installing them. In this chapter, I will look at all the plant categories I covered in part one, but this time in the context of actual planting. Read each section carefully, especially the sections on plants you are intending to plant, as wrong installation can have catastrophic effects on your garden.

GROUNDCOVERS AND PERENNIALS

Groundcovers are a great way to take up space in your new xeriscaped garden. In general, you should wait until the fall to plant these, since the summer heat can scorch them too much. Over the winter, they will gain strong roots so they can blossom perfectly the following spring. Many gardeners advise planting groundcovers in shaded areas, since they are often somewhat sensitive to sun. One of the best places to plant them, then, is under trees. This will help the trees retain moisture, as well as avoid the often barren circle that tends to surround trees in grassy areas. They also act as a natural mulch for your trees, making this planting technique a win-win! Thus, choosing either a generally shady or an under-tree area for your groundcovers will help you avoid scorching, and keep both your trees and groundcovers happy.

(Figure 8.1, *How to plant a seedling*)

The best way to plant your groundcovers is to first loosen the soil. Depending on how recently you put in the ground soil, or if you put it in at all, you might have to loosen it more or less. Evaluate the soil first. Does it look packed or hard? If so, take a fork or a hoe and make sure it is loose down to where you want to do planting. This will make sure your groundcover's roots will be able to grow, and that there will be adequate drainage for your watering. As I've said, many xeriscaping plants are very sensitive to soil water-logging, so making sure they have adequate drainage is a must. Next, make sure the soil is well-fertilized. Many groundcovers need a lot of nutrients to survive, so refer back to Chapter 7's section on fertilizing for advice on how to create that environment. If you are installing pre-grown groundcovers, make sure the soil is loosened to the length of the roots, and that all roots are spread equally. If you clump all the roots together, they will have no ability to capture water. A good distribution of roots is essential. If the roots come in a clump of soil, try to break them up a bit to encourage more outward growth. For seed planting, place your seeds at least an inch deep into the soil. This will optimize for warmth (coming from the soil), but also for sunlight and water access. Finally, you should cover these seeds with at least three inches of mulch. This mulch will keep your groundcovers safe from any cold, especially in cold desert regions, as well as from animals. By spring, your groundcovers should be sprouting wonderfully.

SHRUBS

For larger shrubs, there are some very different rules. Shrubs need a lot of drainage, so any soil that is high in clay or rock content will be difficult for them to survive in. Choose a nice light soil that is very loose to optimize for your shrub's drainage needs. A good way to test soil drainage is to dig a foot-wide hole, and fill it with water. After two hours, give or take, you should be able to see how well your soil has drained. If there is still water left, you probably don't have very good drainage in that area, and thus shouldn't plant your shrubs there. Repeat this process until you find an area with good drainage to plant your shrubs. If you can't find one on your property, you might have to re-grade your soil, adding some drainage-friendly substances so that you can keep your shrubs happy. This drainage-testing aspect to the shrub planting process is essential, as it ensures your shrubs won't be waterlogged after you plant them.

When it comes to the actual planting, you should make sure that there are no leaves or mulch in the area you are planning to plant. Shrubs need to be put in pure soil. Rake or sweep away anything that might retain too much moisture. Once you have done this, you can begin planting. Measure the container that your shrub is currently planted in. Then, dig a hole twice that size in diameter. So, if your shrub's pot has a diameter of one foot and a height of one and a half feet, you need a hole that is two feet wide and one and a half feet deep. This ensures that the roots and the soil that is already in the container have adequate space to spread out. They are likely compressed more than they need to be in the container, and will expand once they are put in the ground. After you have a hole of adequate size in the space where you want it to be, you can put the plant inside.

To remove the shrub from its container, be sure to never pull the stem. This can risk separating the roots from the shrub, which will likely kill the plant. Instead, tap on the sides until you have loosened the soil from the side of the container, and gently shake the plant out sideways. After you've removed it from its container, place the plant in the hole, making sure it is the right height. If not, either push more soil in, or dig a little deeper. It's imperative that the height is exactly right. You should also make sure to rotate the shrub in the hole before you bury it, to make sure that the most desirable side is facing outwards. Once you have the desired height and position, begin to pull the compressed roots and soil apart a little bit, like I described in the above section on groundcovers. Finally, you can start filling in the hole. One of the most important parts of this process is to only fill using the soil you already dug out, as any other kinds of soil can risk disrupting the soil culture. Fill the hole so that the top of the potted soil is covered, and you are done! You have a beautiful shrub that will thrive in your budding xeriscape.

CACTI, SUCCULENTS, AND OTHERS

As cacti and other succulents are warm-weather plants, they are best planted in the late spring. They thrive in the summer weather, so this is the best time for them to grow. Whether or not they can survive outside depends on your climate. If you live in a hot desert climate, they should be fine outside year-round. But, if you live in a cold desert climate, you should be very conscious of the winter temperatures. Generally, cactuses should be kept at a minimum of 65° Fahrenheit, so if your winters regularly drop well below this, you might have to reconsider cactuses in your in-ground garden. The good news is that you can still plant them in large pots, and bring them indoors for the colder months. This might not be ideal for a xeriscaped environment, but if you work hard to embed the pots into the general look of the xeriscape, this can work great. Just make sure your cacti and succulents are kept adequately warm throughout the year.

These desert plants have a similar planting process to shrubs, with a few noted exceptions. Refer to the above sections for instructions on drainage tests and unpotting. For succulents, the drainage is as important as ever. Since all these plants are adapted to extremely dry desert conditions, they are extremely easily waterlogged. For this reason, you need to do a very rigorous drainage test, even more so than for your shrubs. This will ensure that your succulents will have the dry soil conditions that they need to thrive. Another trick you can try, especially if you are planting in large pots, is to poke some clear holes in the soil. This process will also improve drainage as well as airflow to your plants roots and help them stay nice and dry. Many succulents actually use "top dressing," which is a way to both practically and aesthetically improve your plant's environment. Consider using small gravel or sand to create a nice desert feel. Your succulents will look stunning, and most importantly, feel amazing too!

(Figure 8.2, *A diverse collection of succulents*)

For spiky cacti, you have the added danger of getting pricked. The bigger the cactus, the more of a problem this is. In fact, you might have even felt scared of planting cactuses for this very reason! The spikes, the odd shapes, the size—there's so much to think about that even the most seasoned gardeners struggle. But have no fear: There are actually quite a few tried-and-true techniques for planting cactuses without tearing up your hands.

The first thing you want to make sure you have is a heavy-duty pair of gardening gloves. "But," you might be saying, "Cactus spines seem to go right through my gloves!" This problem is likely because your gloves are made out of the wrong materials. If they are made of leather or rubber, cactus spikes can easily poke through. The good news is that there is a useful material xeriscapers have found called nitrile, which is used to coat some gardening gloves. This material is extremely heavy-duty and will likely prevent all but the largest of spikes from penetrating. That being said, you can also try layering multiple pairs of gloves for maximum protection. If you protect your hands in this way, you should be well on your way to having clean, safe hands when cactus planting.

The other technique you can use is to avoid touching the cactus with your hands at all. Tools like tongs can help you handle cactuses in a way that does not endanger your hands. The best thing about this technique is that you likely won't actually have to make any additional purchases. You can use any common tongs you might find around the kitchen. Long, heavy-duty barbecuing tongs would probably work best for larger cacti, but you can get away with small salad tongs for smaller ones. Of course, you will likely still have to use your (gloved) hands for finer details, but tongs can act as a great supplement to keep your hands that much safer. You can also use other barrier methods like towels, steel wool, or any other strong cloths to put more between the cactus and your hand. Once you've mastered the technique of handling cacti using these materials, spikes in your fingers will be a thing of the past!

TREES

Tree painting has become all the rage in recent years, due in part to increased awareness about climate change. This is not just due to mass deforestation, but also due to trees' massive impact on carbon levels in the air. Trees are a natural carbon sink and cleaner. They purify the air and store carbon so that the atmosphere is just a little less polluted. Trees also act as an amazing habitat for a lot of wildlife, meaning that they can help reduce species extinction due to habitat loss. Planting trees on your property might not have a massive impact on the planet at large, but every little bit counts. Plus, trees have many immediate benefits. Depending on their height, they can cast shade on your house, thus reducing air conditioning costs. They can also provide shade for your shade-loving plants, creating a more diverse environment for your xeriscape. The benefits of tree planting are certainly endless.

Fig. 8.3, Desert trees

In terms of timing, trees can actually be planted year-round. However, there are some times of year that are more ideal than others. In general, trees should be planted as far away from summer as possible, so the earlier the better. Early fall can be a great time, as well as early spring. Only attempt winter planting if you live in a region that doesn't really have a winter. Hot desert climates are best for this. If you live in a climate that ever drops below freezing, it's best to wait until the soil has completely thawed. So, depending on your climate, you can actually plant trees at any time, provided you consider ideal temperature ranges.

Once you get to the actual planting, there are similar hole-digging rules for shrubs, only with slightly different proportions. Trees have some of the largest root systems in the plant kingdom, so they should be given plenty of room to spread out underground. The best calculation rule is to measure the diameter of the current root system and dig a hole that is three times as wide. However, like with shrubs, the hole should be no deeper than the current root system already is. This is because burying a tree too deep is very bad for it. You should always make sure that all parts of the actual trunk are still above soil for optimal tree planting. So, for a tree that has a root mass already at three feet wide and two feet deep, you should dig a hole that is nine feet wide and two feet deep. Again, make sure that the hole is exactly the right depth, since you neither want the trunk covered, nor the roots exposed. If you dig the right-sized hole, then you should have a perfect nest for your tree.

One good tip for tree planting is to plant the trees on slightly higher ground than the rest of the garden. This will ensure that the tree's roots have adequate levels of drainage so that they can avoid sitting in a pool of water. Consider either digging your hole on an existing small hill, or calculating your depth differently. You can dig a hole that is only three quarters as deep as your root system, then cover up the exposed roots by creating a mound. If you have piled the soil on properly and mulched it, then your trees' roots will have a perfect environment that maximizes moisture retention as well as adequate drainage. However, make sure that you only fill and mound with existing soil that you dug up. This is because a tree's roots might get too used to your added soil, then not venture past where that soil ends and the native soil begins. This results in small root systems and weak trees. Once you have planted your tree, make sure to only surround it with soil that is in the rest of the ground as well. After that, you can add some mulch on top to make sure it has strong protection, and you will have a happy tree.

BEDS, VEGGIES, AND FRUITS

For the more ambitious xersicaper, you might want to attempt planting some actual fruit or vegetable beds. These projects will likely require a lot more preparation and main-tenance than general xeriscaping, but will give you a much higher return on your investment. For fruit trees, it is best to buy ones that are already seedlings. This is because most fruit trees are grafted from an existing tree, not grown directly from seed. Thus, it is best done on farms that have access to high-quality materials. Many people have been frustrated trying to grow fruit trees from seed, especially if that seed came directly from the fruit itself. Unless you have heirloom seeds and a few years to wait for them to gain matu-rity, you will likely be left with an underwhelming seedling that does not produce high-quality fruit. Instead, you should just buy small fruit trees and plant them in your garden to mature. In these cases, the same rules for general tree planting apply.

But for fruits and vegetables that don't grow on trees, you will need to grow them in beds. Beds are large patches of fertile soil in which seeds are sown. Sowing seeds is best done in the early spring, after the first frost. Different vegetables have different requirements for depth and placement. This usually corresponds to the size of the vegetable. Larger vegetables, like kale, require very distant and deep seed sowing. Smaller vegetables, however, like carrots, can be planted much closer together. Make sure you read the instructions very carefully. It can seem ridiculous to plant tiny seeds over a foot apart from one another, but once the plant matures, it will need this space, and you don't want to risk the root system by transplanting it. You should also refer to specific plants for requirements as to planting dates, with some needing to be planted much earlier than others.

Fig 8.4, Vegetable garden bed growing red kale

Some stray tips for planting vegetable garden beds are first of all to start them indoors. If you want your vegetables to achieve maturity a little faster, or if you live in a slightly colder climate, you can consider starting to sprout your seeds inside before frost is over to get a better yield. You can do this in small, biodegradable containers so that you won't have to actually re-pot them when it comes sowing time. You can either buy these from the store, or use recycled materials like egg carton pods. Another very important thing for vegetables is fertilizer. You should be sowing your seeds in strong fertilizer, but should also continue to fertilize throughout the growing process. Your vegetables are producing a lot of nutrients, and so should have as much nutrients to feed them as possible. If you follow these tips, you should have a thriving vegetable garden on your xeriscaped property.

NINE

installing hardscapes, complements, and accessories

HARDSCAPING IS an essential part of any garden. No matter how minimal or plant-focused you want your garden to be, you will have to include at least a few hardscaping elements. Whether it's just some simple wooden fencing, or an elaborately-designed rock garden, hardscaping is going to play a part in your outdoor space. You might think that you have to hire a professional landscaping team to get the kind of beautiful hardscaping that you see in gardening magazines. While it is true that many of these materials are complicated to install (and even more complicated to install well) you can still do them all yourself, with the right know-how, of course. In this chapter, I will instruct you on how to install various aspects of hardscaping so you can create a beautiful environment which supports your plants.

GROUNDCOVERS

Besides organic groundcovers, you are likely going to need some non-organic groundcovers. These serve both as walkways and as a way to prevent your garden from looking barren, since not every patch can be taken up by plants. A patch of nicely-colored gravel or tile will look miles neater than a patch of bare dirt. Groundcovers give you a unique opportunity to combine the worlds of floor design and plants, creating a harmonious environment of nature and construction. Installing these things, however, is far from simple. Groundcovers especially often require a lot of heavy-lifting as well as special equipment. But, if you take proper precautions and do the right research, you can install them very well. Here, I will look at how exactly to install three main types of groundcovers.

Gravel

Possibly the easiest to install and shape, gravel will go wherever you want it to. Gravel can be bought in bags from most major landscaping or gardening stores, with a huge variety of quality and grain size. For low-traffic areas, you can get away with a coarser blend, more like what you would see in a parking lot; however, for nicer, more sightly areas, you should opt for a smoother blend with a color that's pleasing to you. The main problems you will have with installing gravel are the ground surface and the heavy lifting. You can't put gravel on just anything. If the area you want to put your gravel on is too uneven, consider evening it out with some crushed stone, or coarser gravel underneath. A smoothed out "underneath" will result in that smoothed out "on top" that you're aiming for. For the heavy-lifting aspect, make sure you use wheelbarrows to transport your gravel to avoid injury. No matter how beautiful your gravel work turns out - I promise it's not worth a cracked back, friends.

Patio Stones

One of the trickier methods of ground covering is to use patio stones. They are best used for more formal sitting areas or walkways, since they are a cleaner and smoother ground-cover option. Patio stones can be slightly more expensive than gravel, but there is still a wide price variation. You have the option to cement them in, or not, depending on how solid you want them to be. Otherwise, you can just fill the spaces between the tiles with fine gravel or polymeric sand. For installation, patio stones run into the same problems as gravel with uneven ground. For patio stones to be secure, especially if you want to place furniture on top of them, they need to be one perfectly flattened surface. You can use a combination of crushed stone, gravel, and sand to achieve the perfect base for your stones. Make sure to use a level to ensure that they are perfectly flat. The flatter the surface, the more your patio stones will shine (and your garden too).

Fig 9.1, Patio stones in a xeriscaped garden

Pavement

For the smoothest possible (and most difficult to install) groundcover, you can use pavement. Depending on the size of your paved area, and the depth of the pavement, you might need special equipment, such as an industrial-grade pavement mixer, to install. Consider hiring a paving company if you have a very large, driveway-sized area. However, if you have a smaller paved area, you can get away with doing it yourself. Mix your pavement carefully, following all instructions, and begin laying. You might want to do this in a few layers if your pavement is thick. The most important part of paving is smoothing. Find a large smoothing tool and use it concurrently with a level to make sure your pavement is perfectly smooth. Don't forget to sign your name in the corner—You've earned it!

FENCES AND GATES

An integral part of defining both areas within your property, as well as the property line in general—putting in some fencing, along with gates—is an important part of any garden. The best thing about fencing is that it comes in so many different forms, and can be as simple or as complex as you want it to be. You can opt for a simple wooden picket fence, a store-bought chain-link, or an ornate wrought-iron one. It's all up to your style! From the self-built to the pre-made, there's a fencing installation plan for everybody. Here, I will explore some of the most common types of fencing for gardens.

Fig 9.2, A wooden fence

Natural

You don't have to use man-made materials for your fencing at all. In fact, you can actually create fencing using natural materials, even plants. Shrubs, trimmed hedges, and small trees can all work as natural separators that can keep your garden both visually separated, and in some cases secure. You can go for the subtlest indication of barrier, with a small garden bed, or a heavy-duty line of thick spruce shrubs carved in the shape of a large wall. No matter the need for your fence, you can find a way to use natural materials to achieve it.

Wood

If you can't use natural materials to create barriers in your garden, consider using a more natural building method, like wood. Wood is a very easy-to-use construction material, and for this reason is often a favorite amongst beginners. The most important thing to get right for wood fencing is installing your posts in the ground. You want to dig a very deep hole, much like you would for tree-planting. A fence post that is deep in the ground will be secure, and much more stable.

For fencing, you can go as simple or as complex as you want. Some gardeners construct a simple post fence, which can easily be made using precut wood pieces from the hardware store. However, some home carpenters want to go all out and create an elaborately carved masterpiece which will be a beautiful complement to your garden. Whichever you choose, let it suit your garden's needs.

Metal

You can also use metal materials for your fence. One of the most popular types of metal fence is the pre-made chain-link fence. You can buy these in rolls at most gardening stores, and they can be easily installed. These are a great way to cover a lot of fenced areas very quickly. While this kind of fence might not be as sightly as natural or wood fencing, there are still nice-looking designs you can buy. Besides, the metal fence more than makes up for its less sightly appearance with security. If you need a more secure mode of fencing, especially if you are trying to keep out animals, metal fencing is the best option for you.

LIGHTING

We might like to think of gardens as a daytime-only thing, but they can actually shine very well in the night too. You just have to invest in some great lighting, and your garden will become a magical place of night-time beauty. There are several options for this. The first is to put in some small solar-powered lamps. These can be situated anywhere in the garden, and give off some nice light without the need of batteries or cords. Alternatively, you can install some string lights with an outdoor plug. These are great for eating or seating areas, offering a soft and nice-looking light. Other options might involve more complicated processes like running wires under your soil, or installing timers. These are also great options, but might prove difficult to those without electrical experience. No matter the simplicity, though, adding lights to your garden is one of the easiest ways to send it over the top (and show off to your neighbors).

Fig 9.3, Garden lighting

ROCKERY

Rocks are an essential part of desert landscaping. The beautiful aesthetics of the desert lend themselves so well to rockery. So, no xeriscaped garden is complete without some rocks to accent the plants. Here, I will look at the two different aspects of rockery that will help your garden be the best it can be.

Stepping Stones

Similar to the earlier section on patio stones, another way to form walkways is to create small steps using rocks. These are different from groundcovers because they are meant to create subtle walkable paths through an already covered area. You can use stepping stones through any area that is too difficult or dirty to walk, such as water, dirt, or even thick gravel. The basic principles of stepping stones is that they should be flat and walkable. Short of that, you have free rein. Of course, like with groundcovers, they should also have a very flat foundation. If you are putting them over gravel or dirt, make sure they have a strong foundation, and will not tip over when walked on. Putting them through water is somewhat more difficult, depending on the depth of the water. You might find that shallower water with a sandy base is the easiest, while deep water with a rocky base is the hardest. Gauge your base to see if it's suitable for stepping stones, and as always, make sure that they are flat enough to walk on.

Decoration

Sometimes, you just want rocks as decoration. In this case, solid foundations are only a concern insofar as the rocks won't fall on anyone or any of your plants. But otherwise, make your decorative rocks as unstable as you want! Create rock stacks, mountains, or beautifully-balanced displays to compliment your plants. With decorative rockery, it's all about creativity!

TEN

maintenance

SO, you have an amazingly xeriscaped garden that you are proud of... Now what? Well, now comes the part that separates the novices from the pros. And luckily, this part isn't difficult, it just takes effort. Many will lose interest after the excitement of planning and planting - but for you and me, we care too about the long-term beauty of our desert spaces. This step that I'm referring to, of course, is: maintenance.

The good news is that your xeriscaped garden shouldn't need too much maintenance, or at least as much maintenance as a lawn might need. That being said, there are still some important things that you will have to do to keep your xeriscaped garden looking great. Furthermore, there might even be some garden maintenance specific to xeriscaping that you have not done before, so make sure to read each section carefully to ensure you are maintaining your xeriscape garden to the best of your abilities.

WATERING

"What?" you might be saying, "But I thought xeriscaping meant less watering!" Well, yes and no. Xeriscaping generally means less watering than the average lawn, especially than the average lawn in the Southwest, but it does not mean no watering at all. In fact, you might find watering for your xeriscape garden even more complicated than for your lawn. The general belief amongst xeriscapes is that you should water your garden infrequently, but as deeply as possible. Irrigation can help with this, making your watering even more efficient. The idea behind this rule is that the deeper the ground, the better it will retain water, thus feeding your roots better and lasting longer. If you follow this rule, you should have well-hydrated plants for life!

(Fig 10.1, *How to water vegetables*)

FERTILIZING

We talked about the pre-fertilization process a little bit earlier, but that process doesn't end once you put your plants in the ground. Especially for fruits and vegetables, you will need to continually fertilize your plants throughout their entire life. All the same substances apply, but you will be treating them in a different way. Because you are going to be applying your maintenance fertilizer more shallowly into the soil, perhaps even on top of it, you will need finer fertilizer and less of it. No full banana peels or big chunks of manure. Smaller, natural (and often free!) fertilizers include coffee grounds for acidity, dried and powdered eggshells for calcium, and even human hair for protein. You can also buy smaller, powdered commercial fertilizer for this purpose. The better you feed your plants, the more they will wow you with their incredible growth. One important thing to note: although fertilizer is generally good, sometimes xeriscaped plants are adapted to nutrient-poor soil, so you won't need as much fertilizer. Spend some time re-familiarizing yourself with your specific plants' needs before going crazy on the fertilizer!

WEEDING

Weeds should generally be less of a factor in xeriscaped gardens than on lawns, but they are still a concern. They siphon nutrients and water from your desired plants and can even overtake them in the garden, killing them entirely. Suffice it to say, you don't want them around. The best weed defense is to quite literally nip them in the bud. Remove weeds as much as possible in the early spring so that your other plants have time to mature without weeds, and will thus be more resistant to any later ones that might pop up. They will also be easier to pull out or chemically kill the younger they are. If you maintain this very diligent practice towards weed maintenance, it's possible you could stop seeing weeds pop up within two or three years. After that, you're in the clear to grow freely without the looming threat of these nutrient-sucking parasites called "weeds."

MOWING

For those who opted to keep some (hopefully drought-resistant) grass, you might still have to do some mowing. There are a few drought-resistant groundcovers which serve the function of grass, but do not need to be mowed, such as moss. If you're one of those people for whom mowing grass was a big reason to turn to xeriscaping, you should probably consider an alternative like this. All the benefits of grass without mowing! But if you really like your grass, it's perhaps obvious that this decision comes with the obligation of mowing. Like with a regular lawn, you can just mow to your aesthetic desire. None of this grass actually needs to be mowed, but it can make it look far more aesthetically appealing, and thus is a popular option.

PRUNING

In the tree department, especially fruit trees, pruning is a must. Pruning helps trees keep their shape, not grow too big, and actually sprout new leaves in previously dead areas. Plus, if done right, it can significantly help your tree grow more fruit. Pruning helps clear away dead branches to make way for new ones, and also can manipulate their growth. For those with smaller gardens (or very constricted gardens) pruning is a must, since it will help you keep your tree within your property limits. If you're concerned with your plant's shape and growing ability, you will need to prune. Pruning can be done with a variety of tools, from small hand shears to large, more scissor-like shears. Which kinds of shears to buy depends on the size of your plant, but you should still have at least one small and one large for different branch sizes. As always, the right tools will make your job that much easier.

SEASONAL TIPS

Maintenance is completely different throughout the seasons. Even if you live in a hot desert climate, which doesn't have as much seasonal variation, you should still concern yourself with the time of year, and how that affects your plants. If you live in a more varied climate, like a cold or arid desert, or even Mediterranean, then you should especially concern yourself with the seasons. Planting, watering, pruning, and all the other maintenance aspects that I talked about earlier in the chapter will be affected by the season. In this section, I will break down all the maintenance tasks that you will need to perform for each of the seasons.

Spring

It's an old custom to clean in the spring, but it's for good reason! Spring is a time of awakening, rebirth, and prepare for the coming year. This is as true in your home as it is in your garden. Your plants have just endured a hard winter, and are ready to burst free and be beautiful again. So, the first spring task for your garden is to clean. Clear out all the dead leaves, all the fallen branches, or anything else that might be blocking your plants. Make sure, however, that you wait until after the last frost to do so, since leaves and other debris act as natural mulch, which keeps your plants warm. They serve an important purpose, but once your plants are ready to grow, they can actually block or crush fragile seedlings. So, after you're sure there won't be any more freezing days, you can start clearing your garden to make way for new growth.

The next step to caring for your plants in spring is to feed them, both with water and fertilizer. Watering is most important in the spring. In most climates, this happens naturally. Ever heard the expression "April showers bring May flowers"? But if you live in a more desert climate, and especially if you are trying to grow some non-native plants, you will have to artificially create these "April showers." Make sure you are giving your budding plants as much water as they need, especially if you have had a particularly dry or cold winter. This is also true for fertilizer. Plants need to be fed as well as watered, so spring should be the peak of your fertilizing season. Think of your spring plants like teenagers. They are constantly growing, which means they are going to gobble up anything you put in front of them! Making sure you provide your plants with the proper nourishment will start them on the right foot for the year.

The next two things you will need to do is prune, and perform some basic weed prevention. These two things have already been discussed, but just as a refresher, pruning will help stimulate growth for your spring plants, and help them start the year in the right shape. Likewise, weed removal is best done during the spring, as it kills the weeds when they are young and vulnerable, letting your desired plants mature without interference.

Summer

Summer is a time when you can relax a little in your garden. For the most part, summer should be a time when you just enjoy your garden, sitting in the beautiful seating you've created or having a barbecue with friends. The maintenance you will be doing in the summer is predominantly a continuation of your spring maintenance, but with slightly less work. You are essentially working to preserve the ideal environment that you started in the spring. Generally, you should keep on top of the weeds that might have popped up since the spring. If you did your job correctly earlier in the year, you should only have young and weak weeds to contend with in the summer. Watering should be at your discretion, adjusting the quantity to the temperature, sun, and precipitation levels. The only job you will need to start doing in the summer is "deadheading," or pulling off dead flowers and leaves from your plants. This will become more common as the summer progresses. In general, though, the summer is a time to pull back from hardcore garden maintenance and just enjoy the beautiful space you've created.

Fall

It might seem counter-intuitive, but actually the best thing to do in the fall is to plant! Certain perennials will be coming back, so there's no need to do anything with them, just mulching so that they survive the winter. But if you want to have any new plants in the ground for next spring, you should think about planting some bulbs. The advantage to planting bulbs in the fall is that the soil is much warmer and looser than it is in the early spring, making planting much easier. Thus, they will likely be in the ground much earlier than if you tried to plant them in the spring, and waited until the frost had passed. So, once you reach the fall, besides preparing for winter, you should also start to plan ahead, and get some of your plants in the ground for next year in the form of bulbs.

Winter

Just before winter, you should start insulating all your plants. This can come in the form of mulch, which is spread over your garden beds to prevent frost damage, or in the form of tree wraps, which are pieces of cloth you can spread around the trunks of trees to keep their contents warm over the winter. You can also use the early winter for some late pruning, which will prepare the branches for the spring growth. Lastly, you should worry about water. Your plants need less water over the winter, but they still need some. So, make sure that you water your garden only on days that do not drop below 40° Fahrenheit, and that you do so early in the day. Otherwise, you risk turning your garden into an ice rink, which is not good for you or the plants!

SUSTAINABLE HACKS FOR YOUR PLANTS

In this final section, I'm going to fill you in on some hacks I've learned throughout my gardening & landscaping journey. These tips are like giving your plants healthy steroids. And the best part is you can do all of this with stuff you probably already have just hanging around your house. These tips are a great way to cheaply and sustainably get your plants the nutrients they need.

INCREASED NITROGEN LEVELS

Nitrogen is like a super nutrient for plants. Kind of like how humans need protein to grow - the same can be said about plants and nitrogen. Nitrogen will help plants grow strong roots and structural integrity. Here's how you're going to give your plants a jolt of nitrogen and speed up their growth:

Avocado skins

When you're done with your avocados, you can actually save those skins, avoid the landfill and help your plants at the same time. Blend up avocado skins in a blender with a splash of water (not an exact science, we're just trying to create a viscous liquid). Once you have this avocado skin liquid / paste, mix it in with the soil of your plants. The nitrogen-rich avocado skins will be like a post-workout protein-shake for your plants. You'll be shocked by how much your plants love this! Gauge the frequency that your plants most enjoy, but my recommendation is to not do this more than once per week.

Oats

The same as above can be done with raw oats (if you don't consume avocados). Blend up some oats into a powder, mix it with water and pour this concoction into your plants' soils. Oats contain an incredible amount of nitrogen, and your plants will love you for this special snack. Same as above, don't apply this mixture more than once per week.

CALCIUM AND POTASSIUM

Like humans, calcium and potassium are part of a healthy diet for plants.

Use your excess banana peels and potato skins to create a super-drink for your plants. Cut up your banana peel into tiny chunk, and simply use the potato skins you peeled from preparing a potato dish. You'll soak these potato skins and chopped up banana peel pieces in a pitcher of water for one hour, or longer if you have the patience. The longer this mixture sits, more nutrients will be released into the water. After time, use a strainer to get the chunks of banana peel and potato skin out. Then simply pour the nutrient-rich water into the soil of your plants. You will give your plants an injection of calcium, potassium and other essential nutrients!

INCREASED PHOSPHORUS LEVELS

Your plants need phosphorus to convert sunlight into food better.

Match sticks

Believe it or not, match sticks are incredibly useful when growing strong plants and root systems. What you'll do is dissolve a handful of match sticks in water for 2-4 hours. Then use that water to feed your plants. This creates a super infusion of phosphorus to speed up the growth of your plants.

Or even easier, just directly stick raw match sticks upside down into your plant soil (you want the strike-able match tip to be in the soil). Whenever you water your plants, the phosphorus from the match sticks will get released into the soil and help your plants go SUPER strong.

Combine your application of match sticks with a sprinkle of epsom salts directly onto the soil of your plant. Epsom salts will help your plant to grow, and specifically bloom flowers for plants that offer that added bonus.

RESCUE YOUR PLANTS!

If your plants are dying from too much water (or not enough water) don't give up, because we can quickly remedy this by opening up your plants' oxygen levels.

3% Hydrogen Peroxide
Use 1 tablespoon of 3% hydrogen peroxide per 1 cup of water. Pour this mixture into the soil of your plant, along with a normal watering. This concoction opens up your plants' ability to suck up oxygen and it will

increase their oxygen capacity. It's kind of like giving
your plants a new set of "lungs." You can do this
once every 2 weeks. But you will see amazing results
before that, likely within the first week. Make sure to
trim back dead leaves to make sure this super-water
is only feeding the healthy parts of your plant.

Use a sponge to retain moisture longer

Additionally if your potted plants aren't getting
enough water, you can use a sponge from around the
house and place it at the bottom of the pot. The
sponge will act as a reservoir of water to keep your
soil moist for longer.

Avoid disease and bugs

Spray cooled down chamomile tea (you don't want it
still to be boiling hot) onto the body of your plants,
and sprinkle cinnamon onto the soil of your plants to
fend off bugs, fungus and disease. In addition to their
preventive properties, the nutrient-rich makeup of
both these regular household items will go a long
way in just generally encouraging your plants to
grow.

CLONING YOUR PLANTS

If you have a specific plant that you adore, did you
know that you can literally clone it? Cut off a branch
or paddle of your desired plant and apply a generous
amount of the sticky goo from an aloe leave (or honey

if you don't have aloe plants around) onto the cut end. Plant the cut end into a pot of soil. You will be surprised by how quickly this clone of your other plant will begin to grow its own root system!

There are a number of other foods and tricks that can achieve these same results listed above. Though these have worked best for me, if you simply don't have these things lying around the house, please feel free to research alternative ways to get your plants the nitrogen, calcium, phosphorus and oxygen needed. It's likely you can supplement any of these suggestions with another household item you already have large quantities of.

afterword

Xeriscaping is a revolutionary gardening technique. It transforms desert landscapes to be more efficient and authentic. It puts autonomy back in the hands of the home-owner. It helps save homeowners money on water and other resources. It creates a more resilient landscape for gardeners to protect against droughts. It de centers the lawn and injects a sense of creativity into your garden. It often makes you eligible for certain tax benefits and support. It even creates a more habitable environment for local insects and wildlife. And most of all, it's accessible for many gardeners living in drought-prone areas to implement themselves. There really is no end to the benefits that xeriscaping can give to you and your family, if you give it a try.

There are, of course, some costs and downsides which I have explored. Some people love their lawns, and don't want to give them up. Some people find that the initial cost of starting a xeriscaped garden negates any savings after the fact. Others might run into opposition from homeowners associations or neighbors who aren't knowledgeable about the benefits of xeriscaping. You might also find that the labor involved in installing and maintaining a xeriscaped garden is too much for the average gardener. All these things might be true, but hopefully this book has convinced you that the benefits far outweigh the costs, and that many of these reservations can be quickly remedied.

Over the course of this book, I have shown you how to begin your xeriscaping journey in just a few steps. I have looked at the different kinds of plants that work best for drought-resistant gardens, helping you choose what is best for your landscape. I have also listed some of the most common subsections of desert landscapes, and explored how one might change their strategy on xeriscaping depending on the specific desert region they live in. After discussing these things, I delved into the different tools you need to create your xeriscaped garden, including some hardscaping materials that will help you make your garden into a landscape. Finally, I instructed on some of the setup and maintenance required for having a xeriscape. Throughout all of these sections, I endeavored to give you the clearest possible image of every detail needed to start xeriscaping. It might not be an easy process, but it is fulfilling and every bit worth it for your property and for the environment.

If you enjoyed reading this book, learned something about xeriscaping, or even got completely inspired to start a whole xeriscaping garden, then I would really appreciate a review. Hearing about your personal experience with xeriscaping brings me a lot of joy. It's, as a matter of fact, why I endeavored to take on the challenge of writing this book. Everyone's experience with xeriscaping is unique, and so sharing your story can not only help me improve what I do, but also help other aspiring xeriscapers learn new tips and tricks on how to up their game. If you have any stories or opinions to share, please do so. It means the world to me and your fellow xeriscapers.

You are now ready to go out into the world and start purchasing some gravel, cacti, and drought-resistant seedlings to make into a beautiful garden. Remember: There is no one way to xeriscape. You should make it all about your personal style. Experiment with color, light, smells, and textures. Invent new ways to xeriscape that no one has even thought of yet. Redefine what it means to be a great gardener. Rip up your tired, old landscape in order to start creating truly breathtaking desert masterpieces. You know you can do better than a plain green lawn, both for your aesthetic landscaping and the world around you. By learning xeriscaping, you gain the power to both help the planet and your wallet by ditching the boring lawn, and embracing something more profound: the sublime power of the desert.

glossary & helpful terms

Aerial Roots: You know how some plants seem to have roots that grow up into the air like they're waving for attention? Those are aerial roots! These nifty structures help certain plants, like cacti and succulents, absorb moisture from the humid desert air. Pretty if you ask me!

Annual: When we say a plant is "annual," that means it has a lifespan of just one growing season. In other words, it sprouts up, produces flowers and/or fruit, and then dies all within a year.

Annulus: The term "annulus" refers to the ring or circle that can be found on some plants, particularly cacti. This ring marks where the plant has shed a layer of its outer protective tissue, known as the periderm. It's not just a cool visual feature, it also helps protect the plant from sun damage and water loss.

Arid Desert: A desert region which cannot grow a wide variety of plants due to its extreme dryness.

Chlorophyll: The green pigment that gives plants their color and is essential for photosynthesis. It absorbs light from the sun and converts it into energy that the plant can use to grow and thrive.

Coastal Desert: A desert region that has a saltwater coastline, generally more humid than most deserts, but still too dry to sustain most life.

Cold Arid Desert: A desert region that experiences cold winters, often at high altitudes.

Companion Planting: A gardening technique which strategically places mutually-beneficial plants alongside one another.

Deadheading: The practice of pulling off dead flowers and leaves from your plants to keep them healthy and help them grow.

Dormancy: A natural state of rest for plants during which they slow down their growth and metabolism. This can be triggered by a number of factors, such as changes in temperature or moisture levels. Understanding dormancy is crucial to successful gardening in desert regions, as it can help you choose the right plants and timing for planting.

Drought-Resistant Plants: Plants that have a high threshold for dryness, and can survive without rain for long periods of time.

Epiphyte: A plant that grows harmlessly upon another plant and derives its moisture and nutrients from the air, rain, and sometimes debris accumulating around it. They're like the freeloaders of the plant world, but they can add some serious aesthetic appeal to your garden!

Ericaceous: It's a type of compost that's added to soil for plants that don't like lime and prefer a lower pH level. If your soil has a pH level less than 6.5 and you want to grow plants like rhododendrons, azaleas, and blueberries, ericaceous is the way to go.

Etiolation: If you see your plants stretching towards the light and becoming pale and weak, they might be experiencing etiolation. Etiolation occurs when plants don't receive enough light and become elongated and weakened. To avoid this, make sure your plants get enough sunlight or provide artificial lighting if needed.

Fertilizer: Any substance which adds nutrients to soil. Can consist of compost, manure, artificial chemicals, and many other substances.

Garden Bed: A garden plot which is meant to house vegetables, fruits, or herbs. Can also have flowers. Generally does not include many hardscaping elements, and is intended for practical purposes.

Genus: In botanical terms, a genus is a group of closely related plants that share common characteristics. Think of it as a family reunion, but for plants. Members of the same genus often look similar and have similar growing requirements, so if you're familiar with one plant in a genus, chances are you'll have an easier time growing others in that same group. In the scientific name of a plant, it's the first word that's capitalized. For example, the plant

Artemisia tridentata (big sagebrush) is from the genus "Artemisia."

Grading: Layering different types of soil, such as sand, clay, or dirt, to replicate the ground's natural layering process.

Groundcover: Any plants that will provide wide coverage for your ground. In xeriscaping, this can consist of anything from drought-resistant grass to perennials.

Hardscaping: Landscaping elements that are not living plants, such as rockery, stepping stones, or fencing. Can be either for decoration or practical purposes.

Hoe: Large gardening tool used to churn and loosen soil for planting.

Homeowners Associations: Popular type of association in America where homeowners elect committee members and fund local facilities, as well as create rules about home appearances.

Hot Arid Desert: A desert region which has an average yearly temperature of at least 65° Fahrenheit (18° Celsius).

Hybrid: A plant that results from the cross-pollination of two different species within the same genus (or, less commonly, very similar genera). This can lead to a plant with unique characteristics that might not have existed otherwise.

Irrigation: A gardening technique where pipes are placed in the ground to artificially create groundwater, and hydrate plants through their roots.

Köppen Climate Classification: A framework for categorizing the world's climates by region.

Landscaping: Any outdoor design involving plants or hardscaping elements.

Loam: The Goldilocks of all soil types - not too sandy, not too clayey, but just right. It's a perfect mix of sand, silt, and clay that provides the ideal conditions for plant growth. It has great drainage and moisture-holding capabilities, making it a favorite among gardeners.

Mediterranean Climate: A warm region which experiences both droughts and rainstorms, becoming more similar to deserts due to climate change.

Mulch: Natural insulation which is placed on top of regular soil to keep in moisture and warmth, often over the winter. Can be made of wood chips, cardboard, leaves, or any other biodegradable insulator.

Native Plants: Plants that have existed in a particular region prior to human intervention, and have evolved along with the natural landscape.

Perennial: Plants that can live for at least three years, and thus three cycles of seasons.

pH: It's a measure of the acidity or alkalinity of your soil and ranges from 0 to 14, with 7 being neutral. It's common for desert plants (especially cacti and succulents) to prefer a slightly acidic soil pH of around 4 to 6, but there are always exceptions. Accordingly, make sure you research your desired plants and test your soil to create the best possible soil environment for them.

Photosynthesis: The process by which plants use energy from the sun to turn water and carbon dioxide into oxygen and sugars. Without it we wouldn't have plants at all.

Pinching Out: A technique used to encourage localized growth in plants. By removing the growing tip of a stem, you can stimulate the plant to produce more side shoots, resulting in a fuller and more compact plant. This can be especially useful for plants like shrubs or cacti that can become an undesired shape if left to grow unchecked.

Rib: The raised lines or ridges that run vertically up and down some types of cacti. These ribs are composed of the plant's vascular bundles and are responsible for transporting water and nutrients throughout the plant.

Rockery: Rock elements in a garden, usually for decoration.

Root Ball: The mass of roots that a plant has grown into a compact, tangled sphere shape. When transplanting a plant, it's important to be mindful of the root ball to avoid damaging the roots and stunting the plant's growth. So, handle that root ball with care!

Rosette: A term that isn't just reserved for fancy French pastries. In the plant world, a rosette refers to a cluster of leaves that grow from a central point at the base of the plant, often creating a circular pattern. It's a common feature of many succulents, which makes it an important term for you to know as you plan your arid garden oasis.

Semi-Arid Desert: A desertous region which is slightly less dry and can thus grow a wider variety of plants.

Sheet Covering: A grass-killing method which involves covering your grass in wet cardboard, then woodchips, and waiting a few months. One of the more eco-friendly methods.

Shovel: A large spade meant for digging heavier parts of the garden.

Solarization: A grass-killing method which involves placing large plastic sheets over your grass in order to kill it with heat.

Spade: A small shovel meant for finer digging.

Species: A group of living organisms underneath a "genus". These organisms share common characteristics and are capable of interbreeding to produce fertile offspring. For example, the plant *Artemisia tridentata* (big sagebrush) is a species distinct from other specimen found in the genus "Artemisia" such as *Artemisia vulgaris* (mugwort) or *Artemisia absinthium* (common wormwood).

Succulent: A desert plant which usually has thick, waxy skin and gelatinous insides.

Top-dressing: If you want to give your plants a boost, listen up: top-dressing is a technique where you add a layer of compost, fertilizer, pebbles, etc. to the top of the soil. This can help improve soil structure, retain moisture, and provide essential nutrients to your thirsty plants. Just don't forget to water it in!

Tuber: A thickened underground stem that stores nutrients for the plant. It's a handy adaptation for plants that need to survive in tough, dry conditions.

Zygomorphic: A fancy way of saying that a flower has a bilateral symmetry, meaning it can be divided into two identical halves only along one plane. So, next time you're admiring a flower, see if you can spot its zygomorphic features!

bibliography

Appropriate Maintenance. (n.d.). *Water Use It Wisely.* https://wateruseit-wisely.com/saving-water-outdoors/how-to-xeriscape/appropriate-main-tenance/

Arnfield, A. J. (2019). *Koppen climate classification | description, map, & chart. Encyclopædia Britannica.* https://www.britannica.com/science/Koppen-climate-classification

Basics of Drip irrigation. (n.d.). Cochise County Master Gardeners. https://cals.arizona.edu/cochise/mg/basics-drip-irrigation

9 best drought-tolerant vegetables. (2022, February 13). *Lawn Care Blog | Lawn Love.* https://lawnlove.com/blog/best-drought-tolerant-vegetables/

Bernard, C. (2018, September 28). *Artemisia annua : anti-malaria and anti-cancer.* Althea Provence. https://www.altheaprovence.com/artemisia-annua-armoise-annuelle-anti-malaria-et-anti-cancer/

Best landscape design software for windows & mac of 2022 (free & pro). (2018, September 24). MacHow2. https://machow2.com/best-landscape-design-software-mac/

11 best drought-tolerant trees that laugh at thirst. (n.d.). The Spruce. https://www.thespruce.com/drought-tolerant-trees-2132053

10 best types of drought-tolerant lawn grass. (n.d.). The Spruce. https://www.thespruce.com/dought-tolerant-lawn-grass-2153119

Beyond the lawn. (n.d.). University of California Resources. https://ucanr.edu/sites/sacmg/Beyond_Lawn/

Black Sage, Salvia mellifera. (n.d.). Calscape. https://calscape.org/Salvia-mellifera-(Black-Sage)

Blue fescue ornamental grass. (n.d.). The Spruce. https://www.thespruce.com/blue-fescue-grass-2132481

Build your own natural stone sidewalk. (2019). The Spruce. https://www.thespruce.com/how-to-build-a-stone-walkway-2132040

Clark, A., & Guthart, S. (2011). *Tips and tricks for successful xeriscaping.* https://www.thorntonwater.com/wp-content/uploads/2020/02/tips-and-tricks-for-successful-xeriscaping.pdf

211

Coastal desert biome plants. (n.d.). Garden Guides. https://www.garden-guides.com/12382883-coastal-desert-biome-plants.html

Cold desert biome plants. (n.d.-a). Sciencing. https://sciencing.com/types-trees-grow-jungle-5031331.html

Cold desert biome plants. (n.d.-b). Garden Guides. https://www.garden-guides.com/107305-cold-desert-biome-plants.html

Creosote Bush, Creosote, Larrea tridentata. (2019). DesertUSA. https://www.desertusa.com/creoste.html

Dave. (2008, July 1). *Laying a natural stepping stone pathway.* Growing the Home Garden. https://growingthehomegarden.com/laying-natural-stepping-stone-pathway/

The desert biome. (2019). Berkeley.edu. https://ucmp.berkeley.edu/exhibits/biomes/deserts.php

Direct, A. G. (2020, September 30). *How to remove turf - 3 ways to remove grass.* Artificial Grass Direct. https://www.artificialgrass-direct.com/how-to-remove-turf/#:~:text=Smothering-

Domoney, D. (2014, April 21). *How to: transplant plants and shrubs to new positions.* Dwalsh. https://www.daviddomoney.com/how-to-dig-up-and-move-perennials-and-shrubs-in-the-garden/

Drought-tolerant trees. (n.d.). Agrilife. https://agrilife.org/treecarekit/tree-identification-selection/drought-tolerant-trees/

Dry ground? Drought-tolerant ground covers to the rescue. (n.d.). The Spruce. https://www.thespruce.com/drought-tolerant-ground-covers-2132051

Fire smart landscaping. (n.d.). Ready for Wildfire. https://www.readyforwildfire.org/prepare-for-wildfire/get-ready/fire-smart-landscaping/

Fontinelle, A. (n.d.). *9 things to know about homeowners associations.* Investopedia. https://www.investopedia.com/articles/mortgages-real-estate/08/homeowners-associations-tips.asp

Friedman, A. (2010, June 25). *Names of plants that live in the desert.* Hunker. https://www.hunker.com/13428029/names-of-plants-that-live-in-the-desert

Garden Gate Staff. (2018, February 28). *How to Plant Perennials in Four Simple Steps.* Garden Gate. https://www.gardengatemagazine.com/articles/how-to/plant/how-to-plant-perennials-in-four-simple-steps/

Geodiode - the ultimate resource for world climate and biomes. (2022). Geodiode. https://geodiode.com/climate/hot-deserts

Grass removal methods. (n.d.). University of California Resources. https://ucanr.edu/sites/scmg/Lawn_Replacement

Groundcovers suitable for replacing turf in San Antonio, Texas. (n.d.). Www.rainbowgardens.biz. https://www.rainbowgardens.biz/turf-and-lawn/groundcovers-for-san-antonio-replacing-turf/

Grow the beautiful tropical bird of paradise plant with these tips. (n.d.). The Spruce. https://www.thespruce.com/how-to-grow-strelitzia-1902742

Heusinkveld, D. (n.d.). *Irrigation tips for desert gardens.* Arizona Daily Star. https://tucson.com/lifestyles/irrigation-tips-for-desert-gardens/article_c8ef8002-acf8-11eb-aca0-2b544da8b1a4.html

Hobbiest gardening - growing fruit tree plants from seed. (n.d.). Penn State Extension. https://extension.psu.edu/hobbiest-gardening-growing-fruit-tree-plants-from-seed

Hot desert plants. (n.d.). Crimson Sands Tourism. http://crimsonsandstourism.weebly.com/hot-desert-plants.html

Hot deserts. (2019). BBC Bitesize. https://www.bbc.co.uk/bitesize/guides/zpnq6fr/revision/1

How to deal with weeds in arizona. (n.d.). Wildflower Desert Design. https://www.wildflowerdesertdesign.com/wdd-blog/how-to-deal-with-weeds-in-arizona

How to easily grow exotic passion flowers. (n.d.). The Spruce. https://www.thespruce.com/passion-flowers-1403114

How to grade and prepare soil for building projects: 13 steps. (n.d.). WikiHow. https://www.wikihow.com/Grade-and-Prepare-Soil-for-Building-Projects

How to grow a cactus. (n.d.). Www.miraclegro.com. https://www.miraclegro.com/en-us/library/flowers-landscaping/how-grow-cactus

How to grow the sunburst honey locust tree. (n.d.). The Spruce. https://www.thespruce.com/sunburst-honey-locust-trees-2132048

How to install a stepping stone path that won't kill you. (2017, October 23). Revolutionary Gardens. https://www.revolutionarygardens.com/install-stepping-stone-path-wont-kill/

How to install a wood fence. (n.d.). The Spruce. https://www.thespruce.com/how-to-install-a-wood-fence-5179417

How to plant fruit trees. (n.d.). Gardening Know How. https://www.gardeningknowhow.com/edible/fruits/fegen/planting-seeds-from-fruit.htm

How to plant shrubs. (n.d.). The Home Depot. https://www.homedepot.com/c/ah/how-to-plant-shrubs/9ba683603be9fa5395fab901583638f3

How to plant shrubs: Step-by-step guide. (n.d.). Proven Winners. https://www.provenwinners.com/learn/planting/how-plant-shrub

How to plant succulents. (2021, May 6). Succulents and Sunshine. https://www.succulentsandsunshine.com/how-to-plant-a-succulent/

How to simply and safely install a metal fence. (2018, March 26). Cavatorta UK. https://www.cavatortagroup.com/how-to-simply-and-safely-install-metal-fence/

How to use polymeric sand when installing pavers. (n.d.). The Spruce. https://www.thespruce.com/what-is-polymeric-sand-2132510

How to xeriscape. (n.d.). Landscaping Network. https://www.landscapingnetwork.com/xeriscape-landscaping/how-to-install.html

How to xeriscape your yard this spring. (n.d.). Sierra Blog. https://www.sierra.com/blog/article/how-to-xeriscape-your-yard-this-spring/

Indian ricegrass. (n.d.). U.S. Forest Service. https://www.fs.fed.us/wildflowers/plant-of-the-week/achnatherum_hymenoides.shtml

Jasmine | Description, Major Species, & Facts. (n.d.). Encyclopedia Britannica. https://www.britannica.com/plant/jasmine-plant

Lamp'l, J. (2017, April 19). *How to plant a tree the right way - 7 steps for getting it right every time.* Growing a Greener World®. https://www.growingagreenerworld.com/how-to-plant-a-tree/

Learn how to draw landscape plans. (n.d.). The Spruce. https://www.thespruce.com/how-to-draw-landscape-plans-2132398

Learn the pros and cons of clay brick pavers. (n.d.). The Spruce. https://www.thespruce.com/pros-and-cons-of-brick-paver-1398074

11 living fences that look better than chain link. (2018, August 9). Bob Vila. https://www.bobvila.com/slideshow/11-living-fences-that-look-better-than-chain-link-47520

Mountain Whitethorn, Ceanothus cordulatus. (n.d.). Calscape. https://calscape.org/Ceanothus-cordulatus-()

Native plants - garden for wildlife. (2019). National Wildlife Federation. https://www.nwf.org/Garden-for-Wildlife/About/Native-Plants

Outdoor cactus for a range of climates. (n.d.). The Spruce. https://www.thespruce.com/best-cactus-to-plant-in-garden-4059807

Planting a tree. (n.d.). Trees Are Good. https://www.treesaregood.org/treeowner/plantingatree

Quick & simple guide to planting perennial flowers. (2022, June 8). Stauffers. https://www.skh.com/thedirt/choosing-and-planting-perennial-flowers/

Rebates, free stuff & grants. (n.d.). Austin, Texas. https://www.austintexas.-gov/department/rebates-free-stuff-grants

Removing your lawn. (n.d.). Water.ca.gov. https://water.ca.gov/Water-Basics/Conservation-Tips/Removing-Your-Lawn

Rock gardening easy guide & 5 tips to rock your garden. (2021, March 19). Www.plantedwell.com. https://www.plantedwell.com/rock-gardening/

Salt bush: an Australian native bush food. (n.d.). Taste Australia Bush Food Shop. https://www.bushfoodshop.com.au/saltbush/

Semi-arid desert plants. (n.d.). Garden Guides. https://www.gardenguides.-com/13428334-semi-arid-desert-plants.html

Semiarid desert. (2019). The Desert. http://thedesertbiomeproject.weebly.-com/semiarid-desert.html

Soil improvement. (n.d.). Water Use It Wisely. https://wateruseitwisely.-com/saving-water-outdoors/how-to-xeriscape/soil-improvement/

Soil science. (n.d.). Soils of the Southwestern US. http://geology.teacher-friendlyguide.org/index.php/25-southwestern/620-soils-sw/

Sowing seeds in the vegetable garden. (n.d.). Almanac.com. https://www.al-manac.com/sowing-seeds-vegetable-garden

Southwest colorado wildflowers, chrysothamnus. (2021). Swcoloradowild-flowers. https://www.swcoloradowildflowers.com/Yellow%20En-larged%20Photo%20Pages/chrysothamnus.htm

Stack Path. (n.d.). Www.gardeningknowhow.com. https://www.gardening-knowhow.com/edible/fruits/fegen/planting-seeds-from-fruit.htm

This is what to expect with xeriscape landscaping. (2019). The Spruce. https://www.thespruce.com/xeriscape-landscaping-meaning-2131129

Tips on selecting the right landscaping stone for your needs. (n.d.). The Spruce. https://www.thespruce.com/types-of-landscaping-rocks-5324154

USDA Plant Hardiness Map. (n.d). USDA Agricultural Research Center. https://planthardiness.ars.usda.gov/pages/view-maps/

What and where are coastal deserts? (n.d.). WorldAtlas. https://www.worl-datlas.com/articles/what-and-where-are-coastal-deserts.html

What are the most drought-tolerant shrubs? (n.d.). The Spruce. https://www.thespruce.com/drought-tolerant-shrubs-2132052

What causes deserts to form? (2017). Sciencing. https://sciencing.-com/causes-deserts-form-72188241.html

What climate is landlocked and gets little precipitation? (n.d.). Sciencing.

https://sciencing.com/climate-landlocked-gets-little-precipitation-21799.html

What kills grass and weeds permanently? [*Busting 5 popular weed control myths*]. (2021, April 5). Pepper's Home & Garden. https://peppershomeandgarden.com/what-kills-grass-weeds-permanently/

What percentage of the earth's land surface is desert? (2010, June 1). Universe Today. https://www.universetoday.com/65639/what-percentage-of-the-earths-land-surface-is-desert/#:~:text=Deserts%20actually%20make%20up%2033

Wilson, S. (2022, March 19). *Mediterranean plants – the 10 best to grow in your backyard*. Homes and Gardens. https://www.homesandgardens.com/gardens/mediterranean-plants

Xeriscape incentive program (XIP). (n.d.). Www.fcgov.com. https://www.fcgov.com/utilities/residential/conserve/water-efficiency/xeriscape/incentive-program/

Xeriscape landscaping: Pros and cons. (2022, January 25). Backyard Boss. https://www.backyardboss.net/xeriscape-landscaping-pros-and-cons/

image references

CHAPTER 2:

Figure 2.1. VectorMine. (2020). [Image]. https://www.istock photo.com/portfolio/normaals?mediatype=illustration.

Figure 2.2. United States Department of Agriculture (USDA). (2012). [Image]. https://planthardiness.ars.usda.gov/PHZMWeb/Maps.aspx.

Velvet Mesquite 1. Lpcornish. (2020). [Image]. Stock photo ID:1253684551.

Velvet Mesquite 2. Lpcornish. (2020). [Image]. Stock photo ID:1262046875.

Shingle Oak 1. weisschr. (2020). [Image]. Stock photo ID:1279698197.

Shingle Oak 2. pcturner71. (2019). [Image]. Stock photo ID:1187669568.

Desert Ironwood 1. Jeremy Christensen. (2018). [Image]. Stock photo ID: 907913120.

Desert Ironwood 2. Jared Quentin. (2019). [Image]. Stock photo ID: 1088302474.

Hawthorn 1. guy-ozenne. (2021). [Image]. Stock photo ID: 1300292960.

Hawthorn 2. _Alicja_. (2019). [Image]. via Pixabay.

Desert Willow 1. Grossinger. (No date). [Image]. Royalty-free stock photo ID: 2155581401.

Desert Willow 2. Lynn A. Nymeyer. (No date). [Image]. Royalty-free stock photo ID: 1245582115.

Shagbark Hickory 1. Elmar Langle. (No date). [Image]. Royalty-free stock photo ID: 1981575647.

Shagbark Hickory 2. Martin Fowler. (No date). [Image]. Royalty-free stock photo ID: 334904378.

Ginkgo Biloba 1. iStockPhoto Stock file ID: 1269532951.

Ginkgo Biloba 2. iStockPhoto Stock file ID:1055535566.

Sunburst Honey Locust. Shutterstock file ID: 1741545719.

Netleaf Hackberry 1. iStockPhoto Stock file ID:667578370.

Netleaf Hackberry 2. Shutterstock file ID: 458849710.

Netleaf Hackberry 3. Shutterstock file ID: 1566374299.

Chuparosa 1. iStockPhoto Stock file ID:1140014944.

Chuparosa 2. iStockPhoto Stock file ID:1398196443.

Fairy Duster 1. iStockPhoto Stock file ID:1424837887.

Fairy Duster 2. iStockPhoto Stock file ID:1397516079.

Blue Star Juniper. Shutterstock file ID: 1709014135.

Virginia Sweetspire. Shutterstock file ID: 1117479191.

Strelitzia. iStockPhoto Stock file ID:177088144.

Cotoneaster 1. iStockPhoto Stock file ID:1345163355.

Cotoneaster 2. _Alicja_. (2019). [Image]. via Pixabay.

Beavertail Cactus 1. iStockPhoto Stock file ID:1364867134.

Beavertail Cactus 2. amberdiehl. (2019). [Image]. via Pixabay.

Blue Flame Cactus. iStockPhoto Stock file ID:1072674254.

IMAGE REFERENCES

Candelabra. iStockPhoto Stock file ID:1365167509.

Buckhorn Cholla 1. iStockPhoto Stock file ID:486289743.

Buckhorn Cholla 2. Photo by Manda Hansen on Unsplash

Queen of the Night 1. iStockPhoto Stock file ID:1359796263.

Queen of the Night 2. iStockPhoto Stock file ID:1421230213.

Ocotillo 1. Shutterstock file ID: 1143642908.

Ocotillo 2. Shutterstock file ID: 1117479191.

Cowpeas 1. PaleBlueDot. (2022). [Image]. via Pixabay.

Cowpeas 2. discofeen. (2022). [Image]. via Pixabay.

Swiss Chard. mabelamber. (2022). [Image]. via Pixabay.

Okra 1. elouis73. (2022). [Image]. via Pixabay.

Okra 2. buntysmum. (2022). [Image]. via Pixabay.

Goji Berry 1. Photo by Maddi Bazzocco on Unsplash.

Goji Berry 2. Photo by Frank Dudek on Unsplash.

Sweet Potato 1. Photo by Louis Hansel on Unsplash

Corn 1. Photo by Adrian Infernus on Unsplash

Corn 2. Photo by Adrian Infernus on Unsplash

Angelina Sedum. didgeman. (2022). [Image]. via Pixabay.

Candytuft. neelam279. (2022). [Image]. via Pixabay.

Ice Plant. iStockPhoto Stock file ID:1321502081.

Buffalograss 1. iStockPhoto Stock file ID:1153378387.

Buffalograss 2. PatternPictures. (2022). [Image]. via Pixabay.

Sheep Fescue. iStockPhoto Stock file ID:1264084605.

Wheatgrass 1. iStockPhoto Stock file ID:520556618.

Wheatgrass 2. iStockPhoto Stock file ID:1399314888.

Digging and Carrying 1. iStockPhoto Stock file ID:1288683750.

Digging and Carrying 2. Eco Warrior Princess. (2017). [Image]. Unsplash. https://unsplash.com/photos/ TsOeGUwWzWo

CHAPTER 3:

IMAGE REFERENCES

Figure 3.1. Kumar, G. (2017). [Image]. Unsplash. https://
unsplash.com/photos/L75D18aVal8

Saguaro Cactus 1. hopesrphotos. (2013). [Image]. via
Pixabay.

Saguaro Cactus 2. moremilu. (2022). [Image]. via Pixabay.

Bougainvilleas 1. TeeBee. (2011). [Image]. via Pixabay.

Bougainvilleas 2. 18986. (2013). [Image]. via Pixabay.

Aloe vera 1. PublicDomainPictures. (2014). [Image]. via
Pixabay.

Aloe vera 2. Ingoldfranziska. (2017). [Image]. via Pixabay.

Ponderosa Pine. Logolepsy11. (2014). [Image]. via Pixabay.

Rubber Rabbitbrush. MikeGoad. (2019). [Image]. via
Pixabay.

Big Sagebrush. iStockPhoto Stock file ID:1213274260.

Tufted Saxifrage. iStockPhoto Stock file ID:1208050805.

Snakeweed. leoleobobeo. (2019). [Image]. via Pixabay.

Prickly Pear. monikap. (2016). [Image]. via Pixabay.

Jujube. Shutterstock file ID: 334904378.

Triangle-leaf Bursage. iStockPhoto Stock file ID:1408694820.

Creosote Bush. iStockPhoto Stock file ID:1213274260.

White Thorn. iStockPhoto Stock file ID:1300292960.

Chrysothamnus 1. PxFuel Stock photo.

Chrysothamnus 2. Shutterstock file ID:1604188204.

Black Sage 1. iStockPhoto Stock file ID:1095084582.

Black Sage 2. Shutterstock file ID:1767799493.

Rice Grass. iStockPhoto Stock file ID:1390039993.

Salt Bush 1. iStockPhoto Stock file ID:1322457563.

Salt Bush 2. iStockPhoto Stock file ID:506934643.

Lavender. Mouse23. (2021). [Image]. via Pixabay.

Jasmine. Ralphs_Fotos. (2020). [Image]. via Pixabay.

Passion Flower. Couleur. (2016). [Image]. via Pixabay.

Blue Fescue. iStockPhoto Stock file ID:1314331023.

CHAPTER 4:

Figure 4.1. (2021). [Image]. Unsplash. https://unsplash.com/photos/KpUqK6OABLY

Figure 4.2. Perks, H. (2020). [Image]. Unsplash. https://unsplash.com/photos/Gp78kG_5WLc

Figure 4.4. Arcwind. (2020). [Image]. Unsplash. https://unsplash.com/photos/-OKp-rhSWE4

Figure 4.5. Selfors, C. (2019). [Image]. Unsplash. https://unsplash.com/photos/KSixq7nzXQU.

CHAPTER 8:

Figure 8.1. GreenForce Staffing. (2019). [Image]. Unsplash. https://unsplash.com/photos/bYZn_C-RswQ.

Figure 8.2. Vu, Y. (2017). [Image]. Unsplash. https://unsplash.com/photos/2MNFnPdsGyg.

Figure 8.3. Lee, J. (2017). [Image]. Unsplash. https://unsplash.com/photos/UtI8tQGKr1I.

Figure 8.4. Hanna, J. (2019). [Image]. Unsplash. https://unsplash.com/photos/hvSBya7hX2Q.

CHAPTER 9:

Figure 9.1. Halmshaw, M. (2022). [Image]. Unsplash. https://unsplash.com/photos/xwgkJI4bShM.

Figure 9.2. Mason, P. (2017). [Image]. Unsplash. https://unsplash.com/photos/Xu21TslwRAM.

Figure 9.3. Novantino, R. (2020). [Image]. Unsplash. https://unsplash.com/photos/qFHAOFq8TaA.

CHAPTER 10

Figure 10.1. Spiske, M. (2017). [Image]. Unsplash. https://unsplash.com/photos/sFydXGrt5OA.

notes

NOTES

NOTES

Made in the USA
Coppell, TX
26 October 2024

39221918R00138